ADVANCE PRAISE

"Glen Wood is the thought leader for business leaders in our post-pandemic global economy. His practical and effective 'power of circles' approach dramatically improves overall business outcomes and profit while adding value to society. This is the root of capitalism and critical for the sustainability of any business. Too Big to Care is the blueprint for reimagining your company and a must-read to thrive in this new world."

—STEPHEN KAGAWA, FOUNDER AND CEO AT
THE PACIFIC BRIDGE COMPANIES AND GAMA
INTERNATIONAL DIAMOND AWARD WINNER

"Glen's book is the antidote for confusion and overwhelm over how to implement Sustainable Development Goals and comply with environmental, social, and government policies. Glen's practical and thoughtful approach to elevating companies that both care deeply and compete fiercely is built on a foundation of decades-long experience in business, finance, strategy, and development. His leadership on these critical challenges will have a profound impact on global corporate culture for years to come."

—W. BRAD JOHNSON, PHD, PROFESSOR OF PSYCHOLOGY
AT THE UNITED STATES NAVAL ACADEMY

"In today's fast-paced world, leaders must consider the impact of their decisions on many factors and stakeholders: employees, teammates, their families, the environment, etc. As a business leader, I know the difficulty in navigating these needs. Too Big to Care is an honest, refreshing, and thought-provoking book for those seeking to be more responsible in their response to these needs."

—DAVID SMITH, PhD, ASSOCIATE PROFESSOR AT THE JOHNS HOPKINS UNIVERSITY CAREY BUSINESS SCHOOL, AUTHOR, AND SPEAKER

"If you're in business, do yourself a favor and read this book. Glen Wood, a pioneering leader in the logistics industry, provides a clear roadmap to success for companies seeking to thrive in our ever-changing world. Using the power of a circle, Glen uncovers how moving toward a sustainability model in practices, products, and marketing will benefit businesses and give them a significantly improved chance at long-term profitability. Wood's background in logistics and on Wall Street and his experience building a successful, sustainable business helped him develop this realistic, practical approach for a company's lasting success in today's world."

—KAREN HILL ANTON, AUTHOR OF *THE VIEW FROM BREAST POCKET MOUNTAIN*

"Too Big to Care is a valuable book for anyone seeking to lead their organization toward actual, practical progress in the midst of what can often feel like alphabet soup and PR acronyms."

—NICHOLAS BENES, REPRESENTATIVE DIRECTOR OF THE BOARD DIRECTOR TRAINING INSTITUTE, CEO, AND LECTURER

"Too Big to Care is an important message, and one doubly important in this particular moment: to create a lasting and sustainable model for the future of capitalism and logistics, society needs to return to the power of relationships and sustainable business. Glen Wood provides a clear map of the failures likely for businesses that rely on simple transactional business relationships and only focus on profit. He also provides a roadmap for individuals and businesses seeking to find deeper meaning and sustainable growth in a world of increasing interconnectedness. This is a powerful book meant for anyone seeking to lead their organization forward."

—RICHARD FOLSOM, CO-FOUNDER AND REPRESENTATIVE
PARTNER AT ADVANTAGE PARTNERS

"Working as a senior administrator in academic institutions for over twenty years, I was often admonished to examine the leadership strategies used in the business sector. Now businesses are facing new challenges. With extensive real-world experience in the areas of finance and logistics, Glen Wood believes in the power of capitalism to enhance our lives collectively and individually. He is equally aware of the perils of focusing on profit alone, which he has witnessed firsthand. Wood demonstrates the importance of integrating the focus on profit with an emphasis on values, relationships, and sustainable goals, and he illustrates how that approach can guarantee the success and vitality of the societies of which they are a part."

—FREDERICK W. SCHMIDT, D.PHIL., SENIOR
SCHOLAR AND INAUGURAL HOLDER OF THE RUEBEN
P. JOB CHAIR IN SPIRITUAL FORMATION AT GARRETT-
EVANGELICAL THEOLOGICAL SEMINARY

"*Glen Wood's positivity in laying out how we can all be our best selves—and help our organizations be their best at the same time—is the message many of us need to hear.*"

—TONY KHAN, PRESIDENT AND REPRESENTATIVE
DIRECTOR OF DHL JAPAN

"*The future is here. Sustainable development and ESG goals are increasingly used to benchmark corporate performance, at least among those who buy from, work for, or invest in business. In Too Big to Care, Glen Wood and Tatsuhiko Nakazawa make the case with compelling accounts that company managers must also care, now.*"

—MICHAEL USEEM, FACULTY DIRECTOR OF THE
MCNULTY LEADERSHIP PROGRAM, WHARTON SCHOOL,
UNIVERSITY OF PENNSYLVANIA, AND AUTHOR OF
THE EDGE: HOW 10 CEOS LEARNED TO LEAD

TOO BIG TO CARE

TOO BIG

TO CARE

ADOPT SUSTAINABLE BUSINESS PRACTICES
OR EMBRACE DEFEAT

GLEN S. WOOD

— WITH —

TATSUHIKO NAKAZAWA

LIONCREST
PUBLISHING

TOO BIG TO CARE
Adopt Sustainable Business Practices or Embrace Defeat

FIRST EDITION

ISBN   978-1-5445-4095-5   *Hardcover*
       978-1-5445-4094-8   *Paperback*
       978-1-5445-4096-2   *Ebook*

For our incredible children, and the bright future they represent:

Shiori, Soma, Rick, Alexander, Victoria, Abigail, Joshua, and Angela.

CONTENTS

INTRODUCTION

L et me tell you about a cycle of events that plays out every day in the world.

The CEO of a multinational corporation in a major city in say, the United States, has a conversation with his board of directors about something called "SDGs." He brings the matter to his executive team, and they in turn task their managers with this new initiative. The US manager has never even heard the term, but he doesn't want to look stupid, so he does an internet search and lands on a United Nations web page for Sustainable Development Goals.[1] There he finds a list of seventeen SDGs.

Is this what his CEO was talking about? Because nothing on the page looks familiar to him. These are not the usual goals he's asked to meet. The first goal, for example, is about ending poverty. Since when did his company care about poverty? There's another goal about gender equality and another about climate action.

---

1   You can find the United Nations' seventeen Sustainable Development Goals here: https://unfoundation. org/what-we-do/issues/sustainable-development-goals/. Each of these goals is due to be achieved by 2030—at the time of publication of this book, only six years away.

The only thing remotely familiar to him is the eighth goal: decent work and economic growth. His bosses are always looking for ways to make more money, but what does that have to do with—as the United Nations page states—"decent work for all?"

None of this makes sense to him, but he doesn't want to say that out loud. Instead, he calls the manager in Tokyo.

"We need some SDGs from you guys," he says, praying the Tokyo manager won't ask him what it means. To his relief, the Tokyo manager is familiar with the term. "Esdeegees" is a fairly common word in Japan. It's a hot topic in business circles. The Tokyo manager is even wearing a lapel pin to show his company supports sustainable goals. He doesn't know that "esdeegees" is in fact three letters—S, D, and G—and stands for Sustainable Development Goals, but he's heard the word.

The US manager hangs up, relieved. This is now somebody else's problem. The Tokyo manager hangs up, troubled. Sure, he knows the term, but he is not sure what he needs to actually do to make his bosses happy. What can he do in his day-to-day work that will have an impact on esdeegees? How does he realistically deliver on this vague goal?

A CHANGING WORLD

The world is changing quickly. Technology and social media have enabled a new global connectedness and free-flowing of communication and ideas, changing how humans interact and causing a cultural shift. All of this influences business leaders' focus and how they run their companies. It makes them take a harder look at how they are perceived by the public. Leaders question whether they are supportive enough of their people. They wonder whether they are environmentally conscious enough, and if it really matters. They are also worried about what their customers think about their corporate governance and their brand. Are they transparent enough? Are they too transparent?

Leaders are wondering how the traditional nature of their businesses fits in this new corporate environment. They know what has worked in the past, but fear that the relevance of their established brand is waning. They want to know which parts of their brand are timeless—and which parts are outdated. They are proud of where they came from and believe in the value of their company heritage. But they don't know exactly where they are going and question whether their history will continue to benefit them or become a detriment to growth.

At the same time, the pressure on business leaders to globalize—or not to globalize—comes with a lot of uncertainty. If globalization is the best path forward for their company, they want to know the best time to start, how quickly to ramp up, and how much globalization will be necessary to remain competitive. How will globalization change their company and will they need to change the way they do business to fit into the culture of the global economy? Whether or not they choose to globalize, they want to know what they have to gain and the risks that come with their decision.

Business leaders also have to consider the expectations of their investors, employees, and customers, not to mention the regulators and politicians. For many, the world around them has changed so much, yet they have not—and now they are at a point where they must decide whether it's time to redefine who they are as a company. This means getting back to the basics about what is important to them, their investors, their employees, and their customers. That's a lot of people to satisfy in a super-connected, evolving world. Do they pay more attention to investors? Close shops and go to an online presence only? Should they shift to a different strategy, for example, a mergers and acquisitions (M&A) strategy? Should they hire more people, or look to cut back?

Hindering their action is the fact that many are locked into a corporate structure and culture that's no longer sustainable. This makes it difficult for them to hire and maintain good talent. They have problems with both employee retention and client acquisition. Their customers are expecting more from them, not just in products and services, but in how they manage their companies.

So are their shareholders. Before making investments, shareholders are now looking at the total environmental impact of a company's policies and practices. Are they damaging the environmental ecosystem? Are they sustaining it? Do they define themselves as environmentally neutral, environmentally damaging, or environmentally helping? Likewise, shareholders are concerned about the social impact of a company—not just within the business, but on the world. Business leaders are expected to tackle harassment, eliminate discrimination, and treat their employees fairly, as well as offer a product that contributes to society by adding value. For example, a tobacco company could treat its employees like gold, but it will always fail the second part of the social impact test because its product is, by nature, harmful to society.

Also on the list of shareholder demands is corporate governance. Are business leaders transparent about their corporate governance policies? Are they communicating them clearly to their managers and employees? How accurate is their reporting, and how often do they share it with stakeholders? These three standards—environmental impact strategies, social impact strategies, and corporate governance strategies—come together in what is known as ESG strategies or goals. (If you've ever invested your retirement savings in a mutual fund with an ESG tag, now you know what it means.) This, along with the United Nations Sustainable Development Goals, are now crucial requirements for business leaders. Yet many leaders either don't know how to address these requests, aren't willing to address them, or they do not fully understand the benefits and the risks of compliance versus non-compliance.

Those who have chosen to ignore the cultural shift may be dealing with social problems, management problems, and even legal problems and lawsuits from employees within their companies. Behind the curve and out of touch, they're struggling to understand why what worked in the past doesn't work anymore. Some are running to catch up, but still very much behind. Others are paralyzed with indecision, unsure of what to do next, and getting further behind by the day. Leaders know they have to make changes, but they don't want to lose themselves—or the heart of their businesses—in the process. What is the best way to deal with this vastly changing world?

THE UNITED NATIONS SUSTAINABLE DEVELOPMENT GOALS

The United Nations Sustainable Development Goals, or SDGs (pronounced *es-dee-gees*), are a great place to start for any business looking to develop a strategy for social improvement. These seventeen goals touch on issues of society, environment, and corporate governance and are "perhaps the most comprehensive inventory of what needs to change or improve":[2]

---

2   Joel Makower, "Can Sustainability Save Capitalism?," GreenBiz, March 30, 2021, https://www.greenbiz.com/article/can-sustainability-save-capitalism.

1. No poverty
2. Zero hunger
3. Good health and well-being
4. Quality education
5. Gender equality
6. Clean water and sanitation
7. Affordable and clean energy
8. Decent work and economic growth
9. Industry, innovation and infrastructure
10. Reduced inequalities
11. Sustainable cities and communities
12. Responsible consumption and production
13. Climate action
14. Life below water
15. Life on land
16. Peace, justice and strong institutions
17. Partnerships for the goals

The United Nations SDGs were developed over decades, but only recently codified for their 2030 agenda. At the time of publication of this book, that's only seven years away. The UN has put out an urgent call for action by all countries, both developed and developing. Their dream is to have a global partnership among countries to achieve these goals. Governments around the world have embraced these goals and have called on corporations to take on the responsibility of helping their respective countries achieve them.

This began at the Earth Summit in Rio de Janeiro in 1992. More than 170 countries adopted Agenda 21, the plan to build a global partnership for sustainable development. The movement continued at the World Summit in South Africa in 2002. In January 2015, the seventeen SDGs became part of the 2030 agenda for sustainable development, and they were published later that year.

Some governments incentivize corporations that comply with these goals, and more guidance can be found on the UN's website. SDGs are more popular in some countries, such as Japan, than in others. Large corporations in that country have SDG pins that people wear on their lapels, advertising to the world that they are an SDG-focused enterprise. (See Figure 0.1.)

Figure 0.1

In addition to the United Nations website, companies can get help from SDG consultants and/or supply chain companies like our own (Smart Vision Logistics) that assist corporations striving to achieve these Sustainable Development Goals.

Another acronym that businesspeople should familiarize themselves with is USP, which stands for unique social problems. Companies looking to make a positive difference in society can start by identifying their own USPs. For some, it may be gender disparity, while others may be experiencing a lack of access to clean water or the proliferation of child labor or child poverty in their industry or community. Beginning with your USPs, you can start to build a strategy around SDG growth.

There are also monitors and scores, such as the country risk monitor and sovereign risk score, that can help you discover how your country is performing in regard to SDGs. These are assigned by private companies.

A company doesn't have to solve the world's problems to make a difference. Leadership should be aware of their business's limitations and respect them. Every country has cultural, religious, social, and historical elements that affect the sphere of influence a company has in social matters. The key is to identify what you can change and begin there.

That being said, it's also time to re-examine our perspective. SDGs can seem overwhelming, and perhaps superfluous. After all, what do these goals have to do with a profitable business? More often than not, leaders find themselves asking: Why should we bother? But they must re-evaluate this perspective. For while a company doesn't have to solve the world's problems, it's time to consider that solving *some* of them is the right business strategy. Perhaps it wasn't the right business strategy for the last twenty years, but for the next twenty, it is the clearest path to strong, powerful profits.

As Tony Robbins said: "Quality questions create a quality life. Successful people ask better questions, and as a result, they get better answers." **Ask better questions.** Instead of seeing SDGs as a burden, ask yourself: Will reaching these goals light a fire under my company's profits? Then do your research. You will be surprised by the answers.

HOW WE GOT INVOLVED

We, the authors of this book, didn't enter the business world intending to launch a sustainable logistics company. We weren't thinking about the United Nations Sustainable Development Goals. We weren't thinking about corporate environmental impact, corporate social impact, and corporate governance (or ESG goals) either. More and more, these are the three standards by which companies are measured—not only by socially conscious investors, but also by anyone interested in a company's future financial performance. Though perhaps it's not so surprising that we eventually went in that direction.

I, Glen, was born and raised on a small farm. My father had died in a machinery accident when my mother was pregnant with me. Unable to support herself and my older brother on her own, she moved the family to her parent's farm in Ontario, Canada. My brother and I grew up working on the farm, which relied on logistics—planning, coordination, and implementation—to ensure healthy animals and sustainable lands. I knew that if I didn't feed the chickens, they wouldn't lay eggs. If the pigs weren't tended to, they wouldn't have piglets, and if the land was ruined, there wouldn't be another growing season. Even at a very young age, I was always thinking about logistics and sustainability—ecological balance—and the business of the farm. Things came in and things went out, but nothing was wasted. We couldn't afford to be wasteful.

I was also quite musical. Thanks to the generosity of someone from church who believed in my abilities, I was granted a scholarship to Toronto's Royal Conservatory of Music. I graduated at a young age and even then, I was thinking about the investment that person made in me and my responsibility to sustain their donation through my own actions.

Just like on the farm with my responsibility to the land and the animals, I wanted to be a good steward of the investment in my education. I traveled to China to teach English and music and was there shortly after the Tiananmen Square Massacre. It was a scary time to be in China, and so I decided to relocate to a position in Japan. I was asked to work in Chichibu, a city located a several hour drive northwest of Tokyo in Saitama Prefecture.

There, I did a "homestay" with a Japanese family, learning their language, customs, and culture. I continued teaching English and music, as well as North American customs and culture, to high school students. I also spent time working at the City Hall helping the local government with international exchange projects. Japan has relationships with sister cities around the world, and people visiting Chichibu from those cities often spoke English but struggled with Japanese. Being bilingual, I assisted with communications. I also helped facilitate meetings between the Chichibu mayor and visiting mayors from the sister cities. Chichibu Township, Ogano Town, incidentally, is where I met my business partner and the co-author of this book, Tatsuhiko Nakazawa.

After a while, my boss and the mayor recommended me to a position in Tokyo where I would take on a management role on a multi-national level. As a program manager at CLAIR, which stands for the Council of Local Authorities for International Relations, I helped manage the logistics of bringing in roughly four thousand people from forty countries every year and placing them in locations around Japan. As you can imagine, the work appealed to my interest in logistics.

I also worked with many senior government officials. Eventually, I was welcomed into a think tank. We were a team of about twenty people, mostly politicians, all working together at the official residence of the prime minister of Japan. This was just after the country's economic bubble had burst, and it was then that I had my first real conversations about sustainability. The politicians and business leaders wanted to know how to create an economy with long-term sustainability, instead of bubbles that burst. The minister of education, who was also there, wanted to know how to build a more sustainable education system. He wanted to know how the country could educate children—Japan's future generations of adults—about the importance of globalization, sustainability, and the relationship between the two concepts.

Those conversations made me think more about my own future. I loved managing multi-national exchange projects and working in music, but ultimately, I saw my future in business and finance. So, after living in Japan for six years, I returned to the United States to study finance, global management, supply chain management, and international relations. I earned an MBA from the Wharton School of Business and a Master of Arts from the Lauder Institute of Management and International Studies at the University of Pennsylvania. After graduating, I joined the mergers and acquisitions team at Merrill Lynch at their headquarters in New York City.

Our offices were in the World Trade Center and surrounding buildings, and I lived just a few blocks away. On the morning of the September 11, 2001, terrorist attacks, my coworkers and I evacuated the building. I still remember running down the stairs and back to my apartment and getting inside just in time to watch the towers collapse from my living room window. (See Figure 0.2.)

Figure 0.2

The utilities all went out—electricity, gas, and water—and then the smell began to seep in. It was horrible, and I knew I couldn't stay. I gathered some things into a backpack and started walking. There were no taxis and no public transportation, of course, so I walked to a hotel in Midtown where I'd stayed before and checked in.

Merrill Lynch's offices had been destroyed, so there was nowhere to work. Communication was also a problem because there was no cell phone service. The cohort I had just joined hadn't been trained, so none of us knew what we were supposed to be doing, and even the people who did know what to do didn't have offices and couldn't reach their clients. Business came to a standstill. Eventually they rented some huge rooms at Madison Square Garden and set up long rows of tables and computers. Human resources set up training sessions, and the space was used alternately for training and work sessions. The most junior and senior people sat side by side, learning the business and running it. After a few months, the company restructured and many people were laid off, including my entire team. So there I was with no job, living in a hotel in Midtown Manhattan.

I found employment in the equities division of Mizuho Bank, a Japanese company with offices in New York. Within a few months, I was transferred to Tokyo. There I worked at Deutsche Bank and Goldman Sachs, eventually landing at Mitsubishi Morgan Stanley. By this time, I had fifteen years of experience and was hired on as a senior managing director tasked with rebuilding their global equities team, which spanned from Japan, to New York, San Francisco, London, Hong Kong, and Singapore.

In late October 2015, my son was born prematurely. (See Figure 0.3.) This was an emergency delivery that happened in an overseas hospital. I was caught off-guard, and not present for the birth. The hospital called to say that this was a life or death situation. They didn't know whether he was going to make it, but I needed to get there immediately. As you can imagine, the news was earth-shattering, but there was nothing I could do at this hour. The next morning, I went into work early and waited for my boss to show up so that I could tell him I had to take emergency leave. I explained the problem and showed him the photos of my child in an incubator with a feeding tube taped to his tiny face.

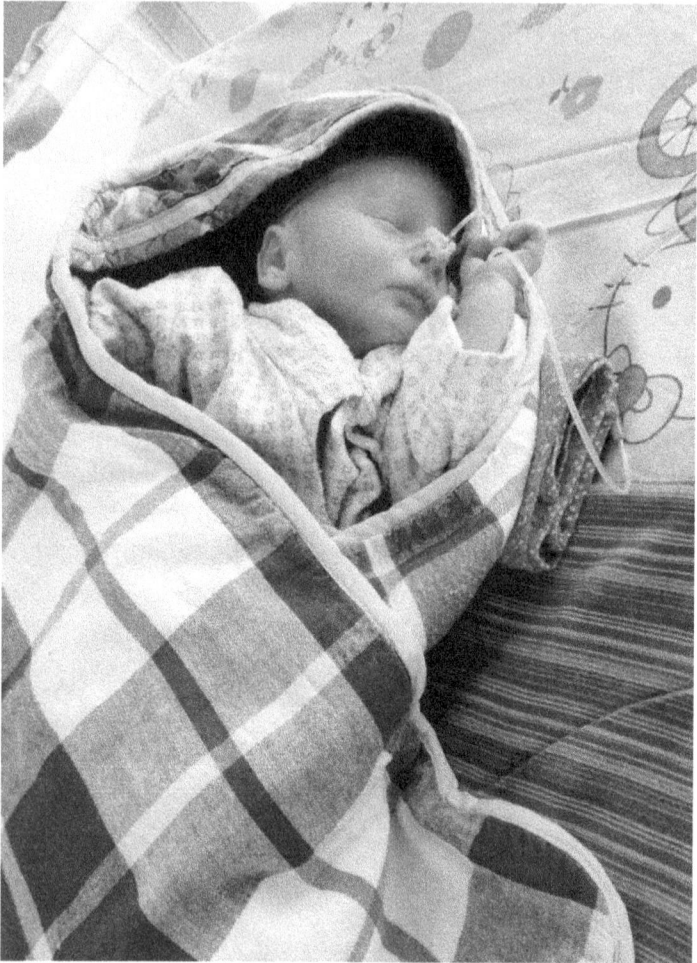

Figure 0.3

Unbelievably, he was nonchalant about the whole thing. He told me that medicine was so advanced these days that I shouldn't worry about my son or my family and should just go back to my desk and get to work. I spent several days trying to negotiate leave time with the company, but they wouldn't budge. Meanwhile, the hospital kept calling, wondering when I was coming. After a few days I got on a plane.

Thankfully, both mother and son recovered. But when I went back to work, everything had changed. You see, in Japan's corporate world, "family leave" is a law on paper, but in reality, that law is seldom followed. I was basically shoved into a corner, treated like a pariah, and eventually fired. That led to a lengthy court battle. In the meantime, I became an advocate for parental rights, which are key to a sustainable company—and a sustainable nation for that matter. That is why, almost thirty years ago, the parental leave laws were established in Japan in the first place.

I found that this wasn't just my problem—parents were dealing with these issues all over the world, and especially in Japan where it's common for people to have to choose between having children or having a career.

During my time in the financial world, I had traveled extensively, and I saw firsthand how logistics operated globally. When I decided to start a business, it seemed only natural to go in that direction. I found the perfect business partner in my long-time Chichibu friend and colleague, Tatsuhiko Nakazawa.

Tatsuhiko, with a law degree from Kanto Gakuen University, entered the international shipping division of Tokyu Corporation in 1998. He began his logistics career driving trucks and working with farmers and suppliers. Tatsuhiko worked his way up the ranks to senior management positions, acquiring import and export expertise and licenses. He leveraged his experience and became the founder and CEO of his first logistics company, TrustOne Logistics Corporation.

In 2019, Tatsuhiko and I cofounded Smart Vision Logistics (SVL). Though I wrote this book primarily in my own voice, I collaborated at length with Tatsuhiko, with his twenty-five years of experience in logistics. As in our day-to-day business operations, our thinking is directly aligned. We knew from the start that SVL wasn't going to be like other companies. We were dedicated to creating a sustainable business that followed environmental impact, social impact, and corporate governance strategies, and treated people as human beings, not just as expendable human resources.

THE HEART OF CAPITALISM

Capitalism is often described as "an economic and political system in which a country's trade and industry are controlled by private owners for profit, rather than by the state." While accurate, this classic Oxford dictionary definition, repeated often in books and articles, does not tell the whole story. Discussions around capitalism may require an understanding of the characteristics of capitalism such as capital accumulation, competitive markets, price system determined by supply and demand, private property rights, voluntary exchange, wage labor, and more components of capitalism. No country's or society's system is completely capitalistic, an important fact to consider in a discussion on the topic. All economic and political systems are a combination of systems, and we label some of them as capitalism because a majority percentage of the country's system is based on capitalistic ideals—largely, this idea of private ownership and property rights.

Capitalism is applauded when it works, but when a country's economic system breaks down, it is often blamed. "People are greedy, and capitalism feeds that greed. Hence, capitalism is evil." This is a simplistic view of capitalism, and a thorough discussion on the positive attributes—along with the shortcomings—of capitalism and its many features is beyond the scope of this book. Instead, we will narrow our focus.

This book is about what we believe to be the heart of capitalism and how it has shifted over time. Companies that have strategic, competitive advantages while following a system of corporate citizenship values thrive in a capitalist economy. The basic principle around which capitalism is built supports corporations that are competitively able to generate outsized profits, while adding extraordinary value to society. Over the last twenty or thirty years, a large number of businesses have strayed from the latter part of that mission.

"Enter the alternatives," as Joel Makower says, "stakeholder capitalism; inclusive capitalism; regenerative capitalism; responsible capitalism; and probably a few others. Each has a slightly different take but a similar goal: to ensure that capitalistic economies and companies lift all boats and consider the interests of a broad range of stakeholders and interests, including the environment."[3] We believe that we must return to this original mission, and to that end, sustainability must be at the core of building any business. This new (or old) business model may be attained through what we refer to as "the power of a circle." Our book is about creating this model through sustainable lifecycles that ensure a mutually beneficial future for both society and companies.

We believe that we're going through a major shift in terms of how the world views capitalism and how businesses work. There's a growing understanding among not only academics and people in business, but also religious leaders and heads of countries that capitalism needs to revert to what it originally was. Many companies have strayed so far from the original intent of capitalism as to render it not only injurious to society, but to the businesses themselves. But the heart of capitalism is

---

3   Makower, "Can Sustainability Save Capitalism?"

corporations' ability to competitively generate outsized profits while adding extraordinary value to society, and business leaders need not choose between these larger concerns and the heart of the enterprise.

You can't have a company generating outsized profits but destroying the environment, nor can you have a business that is planting trees but running at a loss. It's when you integrate these goals that the magic happens, and that magic is what capitalism is really all about. A company that employs poor governance, damages the environment, destroys families, or covers up scandals does not add value, and it is not sustainable. These issues are common and obvious, yet companies consistently follow unsustainable practices for short-term profit that benefits few, at the expense of many. If we simply followed the original principles of capitalism, if we let that magic happen, then the vast majority of our global issues like inadequate food supplies, education, housing, and healthcare—essentially those 17 SDGs—would be resolved (Figure 0.4).

Figure 0.4

This doesn't mean that capitalism is about generating profit in a vacuum. At its best, profit-taking generates value for a society. An ideal and sustainable economy is competitive on the global stage and adds value in ways that are strategically competitive versus other economies. But it also feeds society and addresses social needs. An ideal economy *is* sustainable. It is transparent from the top down, makes people's lives better, and protects the environment. Once you make these elements the focus of the economy, then GDP is automatically maximized. Again, this is the magic of capitalism.

Although people are beginning to grasp this, progress is slow. The United Nations' 17 SDGs is one example among many. Perhaps one of the most surprising is the Vatican's new Council for Inclusive Capitalism, which describes itself as "a movement of the world's business and public sector leaders who are working to build a more inclusive, sustainable and trusted economic system."[4] In their press release, the Vatican says that the council is a reflection of "the urgency of joining moral and market imperatives to reform capitalism into a powerful force for the good of humanity."[5]

Tatsuhiko and I share that vision. When we started our logistics business, we saw the challenges other businesses were facing. We wanted to create a company for today's world, not the past, and we found guidance from many sources. Though we believe that all industries have been affected by this cultural shift, logistics has been especially impacted. Logistics has been transformed by truck capacity and trailer design, as well as technological developments such as new fuels, IT systems,

---

4   Makower, "Can Sustainability Save Capitalism?"

5   Makower, "Can Sustainability Save Capitalism?"

transportation management systems (TMS), and by the incredible growth in demand for logistics services globally.

This demand existed prior to the 2020 pandemic, but the global impact of COVID-19 increased and accelerated the demand for online purchasing that often relied on delivery services. Consumers want products faster and they want them delivered quickly. But many challenges lie ahead. For example, many first world countries may soon face a shortage of delivery drivers. In Japan alone, it is estimated that there will be a shortage of 240,000 drivers by 2027.[6]

The more questions we asked about creating a sustainable business, the more we realized that many of the answers could not be found in other places—but rather, they had to come from business leaders. And so, we asked them: What is the future of this business? How do we build a company today that will be extraordinarily successful tomorrow? What shifts have we seen in capitalism, which ones should we adopt and which should we eschew? What do we want the core of our company to be? What are we and the businesses we represent promising to our clients, and how can we fulfill that promise, while satisfying our investors, employees, and customers?

Our solution began with a basic principle that not only spoke to our sensibilities, but it also reflected the true intentions of capitalism in its highest form: to generate outsized profits, while adding extraordinary value to society. As Joel Makower observes:

All of these efforts to tame capitalism's worst impulses stem from the basic tenets of sustainability—full-spectrum sustainability,

---

6   Yasuhiko Seki, "Realizing a Sustainable Society by Overcoming the Logistics and Agricultural Crises," *Vegetable Information* (January 2020), https://vegetable.alic.go.jp/yasaijoho/senmon/2001_chosa03.html.

that is, not just the environmental stuff: That economies, and the companies and institutions that drive them, must ensure that their benefits extend broadly and deeply through society, and that they promote the well-being and prosperity of all living systems and species, human and not.[7]

If we focused on our contributions to the world, we could become part of the solution to this growing corporate dilemma, instead of adding to the problems. Instead of rewarding actions that benefit a few at the expense of the many, our model makes everybody owners in the company, incentivized to do what's right for everyone in the long term instead of only for themselves, in the short term.

THE POWER OF CIRCLES

Ironically, doing what's right for investors, employees, and customers makes the company more sustainable in the long term. We came to see this phenomenon as the power of circles, where, rather than seeing each process as a linear and finite set of actions with uncertain—and often, destructive—outcomes, we look at each process as a cycle with a beneficial outcome that contributes to society, in effect, benefiting the individual and their business. A company takes from the world: It takes capital resources to pay for everything it needs to stay in business, natural resources to create its products, and human resources to do the work. The power of circles considers the lifecycles of all of these resources. It does not see them as resources to be depleted and cast off, but as sources of continuous value within their company and in the world.

---

7   Makower, "Can Sustainability Save Capitalism?"

The power of circles is a mighty force for changing your goals and strategies. It can transform your management style, your relationship with customers, and your company's social policies. It can guide you to becoming a leader in a changing world where sustainability and profitability aren't mutually exclusive, but rather wholly dependent on one another for a company's lasting success.

Our work exposed us to many other companies—vendors, partners, and customers—that were concerned with their own sustainability. That demand brought us to begin documenting what we knew, and eventually brought us to writing this book. We wanted to share what we've learned about how the world is being transformed, how capitalism is changing, and how companies must adapt to survive. "All truths are easy to understand once they're discovered," Galileo said. "The point is to discover them." This is what we hope to do in this book: uncover the truth about sustainability and what it means to transform a business into a sustainable organization with a durable future. In doing so, we hope we can present a roadmap for corporations to achieve success. We believe those that are willing to embrace this roadmap will win, while those who remain resistant will become irrelevant.

Let me say up front that you will encounter negative examples describing the challenges that Japanese businesses face in the coming chapters. This is simply because it is where I've lived and worked for most of my life, and so it is the country I know best.

I share the sentiments of my dear friend Karen Hill Anton who writes in *The View From Breast Pocket Mountain*:[8]

---

8   Karen Hill Anton, *The View From Breast Pocket Mountain: A Memoir* (Tucson, AZ: Senyume Press, 2020), 273.

Japan has changed me, and although I wouldn't call it a metamorphosis, I can say that I am simply not the same person who came here all those many years ago. Considering some of the difficulties I've faced, it's not that the question "What am I doing in Japan?" never crossed my mind—it's just that is doesn't anymore.

No one is more surprised than I am how comfortable I became in this country. I wouldn't have imagined in a thousand years that I'd find in Japan so much that reflects my deepest sensibilities...

I wouldn't have thought that in this ancient country with all its old customs and formalities and daily obligations, its many written and unwritten rules, I would develop feelings of such deep attachment.

This is how I feel as well. Obviously, this is not a Japan-bashing book—quite the opposite. In fact, I could live anywhere in the world and yet I choose to live in Japan because this is where my heart is. I want nothing more than to see Japan and Mitsubishi succeed beyond our wildest dreams.

And in many ways, even though Japan has a ways to go before it becomes sustainable, its progress is to be congratulated. Fifty to sixty years ago, Japanese farmers were selling their daughters into prostitution to survive, and now we have Japanese companies like Marui that are global leaders in sustainability and SDGs. That is incredible. From being decimated in the Second World War, Japan has emerged as the world's second-largest economy. It shows astonishing momentum, and we can't disregard these aspects when we talk about where countries are at in relation to SDGs. If you think about where the US or Canada were sixty years ago and where they are now with regard to sustainability, Japan's story is a success story. So yes, there are examples of where Japan needs to improve, but these examples can be found around the world.

UNLOCKING JAPAN: THE DATA

To many looking on from the outside, Japan represents a utopian destination: an idealistic society that is to be revered and aspired to. They see a veneer of so-called peace, of dignity, of cleanliness, of incredible efficiency, of "niceness," of politeness, of extraordinary beauty, and of safety. Few stop to ask the crucial questions: Is this really true? What is the cost of such a utopia? Are there human rights in that environment? What are the realities?

- One of the **LOWEST BIRTH RATES** in the world (Figure 0.5)
- Incredibly high **SUICIDE** rates[9]
- **250 PERCENT** debt-to-GDP ratio[10]
- One of the **LOWEST LEVELS OF EQUALITY** for women and one of the lowest percentages of women in management in the world (Figure 0.6)
- **96 PERCENT** conviction rate for anyone arrested, showing just how corrupt the justice system is[11]
- One of the **lowest levels of English proficiency** in the world (Figure 0.7)

We have all heard that if it looks too good to be true, it likely is! And certainly this image of "utopian" Japan would fall in that bucket. I remember very clearly the advice a dear friend shared with me when I first came to Japan. He said, "Japan is a fantastic

9   "Age-Standardized Suicide Rates (per 100,000 Population)," World Health Organization, accessed March 29, 2021, https://www.who.int/data/gho/data/indicators/indicator-details/GHO/age-standardized-suicide-rates-(per-100-000-population)?bookmarkId=bb75d0be-cd45-4d40-8474-d5ade4e72258.

10 Leika Kihara and Tetsushi Kajimoto, "Japan's Debt Time Bomb to Complicate BOJ Exit Path," Reuters, February 10, 2023, https://www.reuters.com/markets/asia/japans-debt-time-bomb-complicate-boj-exit-path-2023-02-10/.

11 J. Mark Ramseyer and Eric B. Rasmusen, "Why Is the Japanese Conviction Rate So High?" *Journal of Legal Studies*, 30 (1): 53–88, doi:10.1086/468111.

place to visit, a nice place to live, but an absolutely dreadful place to work." The experiences of many over the years have revealed this to be true indeed. Workers in Japan pay an unbelievable price to support this system and mirage of utopia.

For example, I would encourage the reader to examine the tax and social security system in Japan. Workers in Japan pay an extraordinary cost to support this system. There are taxes, double taxes, and triple taxes—from property tax to consumption tax, transportation-related taxes, death taxes, asset taxes, gasoline taxes, alcohol taxes, etc. The list is virtually endless, and they are always coming out with a new tax. The lifetime tax and social security costs basically mean giving everything up to the system.

I remember vividly the story of a salaryman who worked incredibly hard his whole life. He was finally able to buy a small home with a two-hour commute to his job in Tokyo. Shortly after he bought it, he had a heart attack from overwork. His family then had to sell the home to pay the inheritance tax they owed. In the end, he worked a lifetime and was left with nothing.

These stories are all too common. The original intention of the death tax was to level the playing the field—to assure that "everyone" paid and that any family legacy wealth would be diminished after at most three generations, leaving everyone at the same place. Corruption, however, has prevailed, and the rich, elite, royalty classes continue to get richer as the average person gets poorer. The elite manage to avoid these death taxes by storing wealth offshore, by using corporations, or by simple good ol' corruption. The local governments, the politicians, and the mafia are closely tied together, which has proven to be a great tax shelter for them.

The tax system is just one example of many that could be cited to explain the extraordinary costs paid by workers to support this system. The above data and the following charts give you a quick summary of some of the drastic results of this system. They show you where Japan is today:

JAPAN BIRTH RATES PLUNGE TO RECORD LOWS AS POPULATION CRISIS DEEPENS
(CURRENTLY LOWEST IN RECORDED HISTORY)

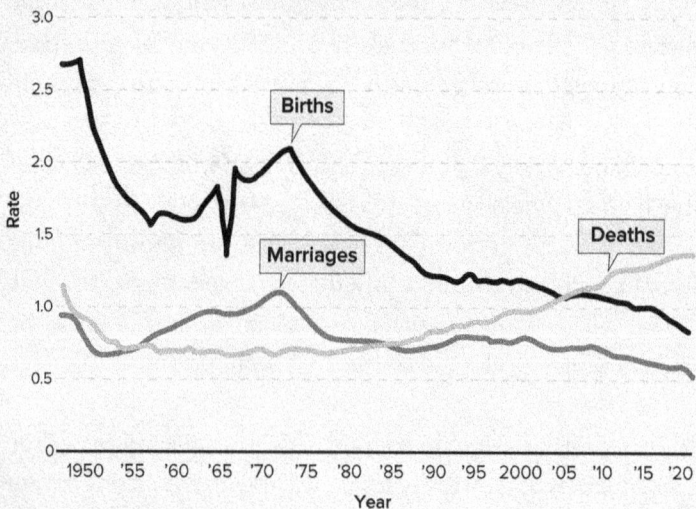

Figure 0.5

WORLD RANKING OF WOMEN IN LEADERSHIP

Japan Ranks **Worst** in the G7 and 121st in the World

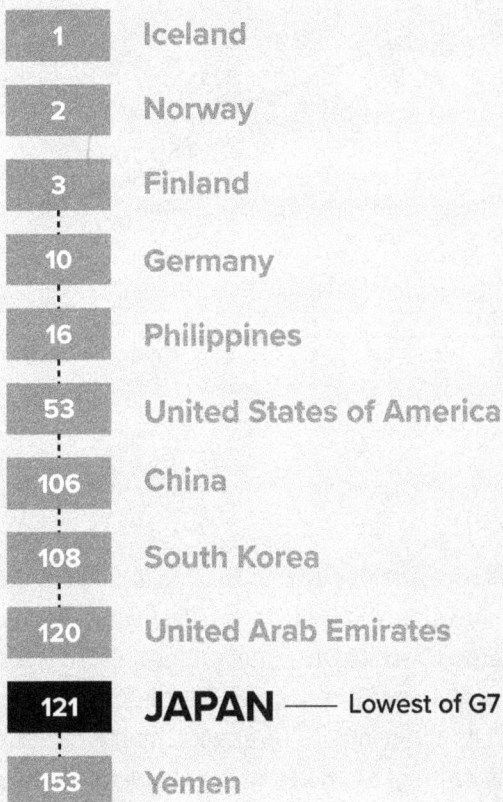

1	Iceland
2	Norway
3	Finland
10	Germany
16	Philippines
53	United States of America
106	China
108	South Korea
120	United Arab Emirates
121	**JAPAN** —— Lowest of G7
153	Yemen

Figure 0.6

JAPAN DROPS TO 80TH IN GLOBAL ENGLISH PROFICIENCY REPORT—LOWEST EVER

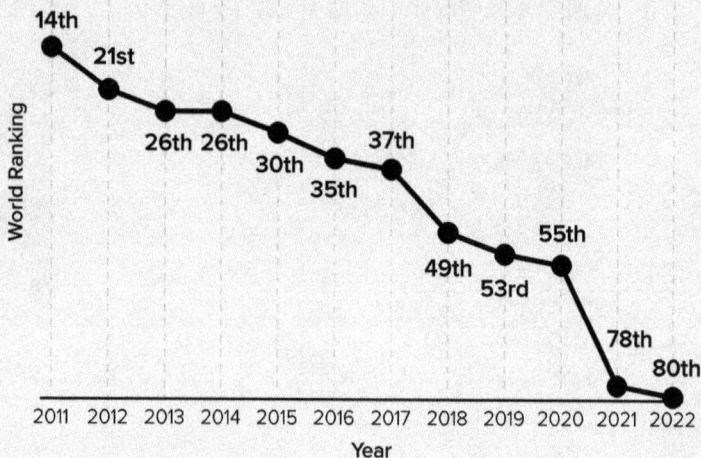

Figure 0.7

As I have expressed throughout this book, some of my dearest friends in the world are here in Japan. I fear these beautiful people have emerged despite the system rather than because of the system. I am hopeful for a brighter, freer future for Japan. I want Japan and its companies to be extraordinarily successful, and I want the citizens of this great country to be fulfilled and happy.

But what will become clear in this book is that countries and corporations *do* need to improve. If they don't, they will be forced to embrace defeat. This isn't simply a theory—it is substantiated by our years in logistics and other industries. In his 2009 book, Andrew Ross Sorkin analyses companies that believed they were too big to fail until the Great Financial Crisis of 2007–2008 hit. You would think the world would have learned its lesson, but there are companies today that still think they're too big to fail. Their size, they imagine, protects them from everything. But their size itself can be an indication of a corrupt and unsustainable way of operating. "Size, we are told, is not a crime," Louis Brandeis wrote in 1914. "But size may at least become noxious by reason of the means through which it was obtained, or the uses to which it is put."[12]

Size won't protect them, just as it didn't protect Lehman Brothers, or Bear Sterns, or Enron. What may save them is adopting the roadmap we describe in this book. If they embrace Sustainable Development Goals (SDGs) and if they implement sustainable profit-generating strategies, then they will be empowered to make better choices to move towards sustainability. And not only will that ensure their success, but it will create a more sustainable economy. But we fully believe, as the title says, that corporations that do not pay attention to the issues outlined here will constantly court failure.

In the end, the challenges facing businesses around the world can only be addressed by returning to the heart of capitalism and seeking to competitively generate outsized profits while adding extraordinary value to society. We believe that

---

12 Louis D. Brandeis, *Other People's Money and How the Bankers Use It: The Classic Exposure of Monetary Abuse by Banks, Trusts, Wall Street, and Predator Monopolies* (New York: Frederick A. Stokes Company, 1914), 163.

by returning to that mission, any leader can transform their company and succeed, sustain, and thrive in this decade and the next. For many, it may be the only hope for the future of their business.

CHAPTER 1

LOGISTICS AND CAPITALISM

"He who rejects change is the architect of decay."

—HAROLD WILSON

At its core, logistics is how physical items are transported from point A to point B, but it is much more than that. Without logistics, there would be no airlines, no mail, and no internet, to name just a few of the services people rely on in their everyday lives. Without logistics, you could order a new tablet for yourself or a videogame for your kid, but it wouldn't be delivered. It wouldn't even be in stock. You could go grocery shopping, but the shelves would be empty. Without logistics, Disneyland wouldn't exist. There would be no rides, no food, and no parking lot, for that matter.

The underlying and often unseen backbone of businesses worldwide, logistics is vital to capitalism. The concept of sustainability that has now permeated our society brings new requirements to capitalism for all, and more specifically, to the business of logistics. If capitalism and logistics do not adapt to this new reality that sustainability has brought, they risk failure.

LOGISTICS OF YEARS PAST

In the past, business was done face-to-face. Business owners and leaders saw their customers' faces. They saw the faces of their employees, knew their names, and knew their families. Businesses and the people who owned them were part of a community, and they felt a moral responsibility to the environment, culture, and people of those communities. When you had those kinds of relationships, you wouldn't fire an employee because he was sick, or she became pregnant. You had to face those people every day. They were your neighbors, and your lives were intertwined. Companies were important to the communities in which they resided and did business, and those communities mattered to the companies. If you treated an employee or customer poorly, there were repercussions. You would not be welcome in your community for long.

As companies grew, adding layers of management that separated owners and leaders from their employees and customers, companies lost sight of their people and communities. Distributed work forces and globalization further separated companies from their people and communities. A senior manager might make the decision to let someone go without ever looking that person in the face, seeing their work, or understanding their situation. They don't know whose life they're affecting, or how letting the person go will affect the individual's team, department, family, or community. The impersonal nature of business today makes hard decisions like that easier for companies to make, unfortunately, because the people who make them aren't emotionally invested in the person. They don't have to think about the impact of their decision, because they don't see the person, and aren't part of that person's community.

Capitalism began with its heart in the right place, but due to a number of factors, became perverted. And while logistics helped companies grow, generate outsized profits, and add extraordinary value to society, the business of logistics also had a hand in its eventual fall from grace. Logistics allowed resources to be transported across long distances, so a company's inputs and outputs didn't have to come from—or be delivered to—a business's own community. It allowed companies to set up sites in remote locations and hire workers who weren't the leaders' neighbors. Without that sense of community, businesses could operate free from—or at least, out of sight of—the social expectations that come with working and living among one's employees and customers.

We don't expect businesses to "go back in time." They're not getting smaller or less distributed, and we can't expect them to self-correct organically. However, some companies (sustainable corporations) are leaning into Sustainable Development Goals (SDGs) and environmental impact strategies, social impact strategies, and corporate governance strategies (in other words, sustainable profitability strategies). That process has started, and logistics is a critical contributor. Modern logistics leaders (including ourselves) see this transition as extremely pro-capitalism, and we believe this newfound focus may be the mechanism that returns capitalism to its original intent.

Capitalism is the best economic system in the world when it's maintained ethically and sustainably. Unchecked, it creates wealth while damaging society. Unchecked, the strategy is short sighted, the benefits, short lived. With a common set of values such as those set forth by SDGs and environmental impact, social impact, and corporate governance strategies, capitalism has a chance to reinvent itself as a force for good, enjoying sustainable, long-term wealth.

LOGISTICS, CAPITALISM, AND
THE POWER OF CIRCLES

A circle represents eternity. There's no beginning and no end. Likewise, a circular business structure with no beginning or end is one that's everlasting. There's always a next step in each process, and inputs and outputs are considered within the cycle. Circular transactions eliminate redundancy and are more efficient too.

In business and logistics, a linear transaction's focus is to get a product from point A to point B. It doesn't consider the effects of using resources to create the product, or of creating the product and getting it to its final destination. It doesn't concern itself with what happens to that product after it reaches point B either.

A circular business and logistics structure looks at the whole cycle and considers the social and environmental effects of its choices. This holistic outlook, as we'll see throughout the book, provides greater profits because business leaders can leverage the power of circles to out-maneuver the competition, maximize their resource utilization, and create a healthy and sustainable business ecosystem in which they can thrive.

RISKS TO BUSINESSES UNWILLING TO CHANGE

Businesses that are unwilling to adopt more sustainable methods will have a hard time keeping up with the competition. The inefficiencies of linear business models will increase costs, which they'll have to pass on to the consumer as higher prices. If they seek to compete on price, their margins will shrink, leading to smaller profits. That means less money to invest in research and development, infrastructure, and other investments to improve the company and its products and services.

The brands of companies that follow an unsustainable model will also suffer. They will be seen as behind the times, out of date, and out of touch with the rest of the world. A business that's less friendly to society, the environment, and investors will take a blow to its reputation, and that will impact sales. The repercussions can be drastic, causing a business and its brand to become irrelevant. People won't want to be associated with them, as investors, employees, or customers. This will impact the cost of capital, of hiring and retaining talent, and of sales. Moreover, regulations will also be harder to meet, especially as their regularity bodies tighten regulations to force more sustainable practices on businesses. Companies operating under unsustainable business models, by ignoring those regulations, will find themselves facing legal problems.

Some of the world's biggest brands have been tainted by stories of child labor, firing new parents, unsafe work environments, and low wages. Those news events impact sales, marketing, and advertising costs.

BENEFITS TO BUSINESSES WILLING TO CHANGE

A company that implements sustainable practices lowers the risks associated with not implementing them, and there are advantages to being an early adopter. Companies leading the way in this direction will get a jump on their competitors and it will be difficult for others to catch up. The sooner a company moves in this direction by building sustainability into their practices and reflecting it in their products and their marketing, the better chance they will have of a long, profitable future.

McDonald's UK, for instance, has already figured this out. For several years now, they have been implementing a series of measures that maximize their resources and eradicate waste.

A great example of this is leftover oil. One of the biggest pain points for fast food companies is, what do you do with all the dirty oil? Almost everything is fried, so there is definitely a ridiculous amount of cooking oil. Where does it go once you use it? Most companies either dump it in a landfill or use it in the production of chicken feed (nuggets, anyone?) but McDonald's UK came up with a unique solution: they recycle it into biodiesel and run their trucks on it. Not only does this lower company costs, but it also lowers the environmental damage of the oil.

In some countries, there are tax incentives available to companies that adopt sustainable practices, especially companies that are friendly to the environment. Those incentives can have a beneficial impact on a company's finances. A profitable company is going to be more attractive to investors and employees, and a more positive attitude in the workplace can impact customer satisfaction and sales.

Imagine running a business where capital is cheaper and easier to come by, one where people are beating down your door to work for you. Imagine one where customers see your brand as a symbol that reflects their values. How much easier might it be to procure contracts with partners and vendors? What about real estate deals for your properties? And how do you think the media will treat your company? Companies want to associate with reputable companies. They want to work with sustainable businesses that care about people and the environment—businesses that get the right kind of attention and will be around for many years.

Thinking that any short-term investments required to put a business in that position will have an adverse effect is simply short-sighted thinking. Forward-thinking businesspeople have already seen the cultural shift and are making changes necessary to thrive in this environment.

The definition of good corporate citizenship has changed. In the past, a good corporate citizen was profitable. How they made money didn't matter, as long as they stayed out of trouble. Today, people are taking a closer look. They have higher expectations for businesses. Making money and staying out of trouble isn't enough—people expect companies to proactively seek opportunities to add value to society and benefit the world in some way.

KEY TAKEAWAY

Capitalism and logistics are in a state of transformation that impacts business, leaders, and the people associated with business, from investors to employees and their families to customers. That transformation affects the communities in which businesses operate, and the places where their resources come from, and their finished products end up.

Corporate citizenship has changed and continues to evolve. Much like the power of circles illustrates the structure of a sustainable business, it also reflects the attitudes of a sustainable leader, one who sees themselves as having a lasting impact on a business, its investors, employees, and customers, long after that leader's career has ended.

At this stage, consider your current situation. As you read the coming chapters, think about how you and your business operate, how much you've changed, and how much more you can do to meet the expectations of this changing world.

GUIDED REFLECTIONS:

1. What is your definition of a good corporate citizen? How have you seen that definition change during your career?

....

2. Think about the types of employees you need to hire now and retain. What is your company doing to attract that talent and make them want to stay with your business? How can you make them feel like fans instead of only employees?

....

3. Are you able to hire "fans" or just people trading time for money?

....

4. How will your business need to evolve to remain competitive, and where do you fit in that evolution?

....

5. What are your competitors doing to attract your ideal investors, employees, and customers that you are not?

....

6. Now that you've read this first chapter, what specific risks do you see for your business, and what are the potential benefits available to you?

....

7. How might you increase efficiency and profitability by leveraging the power of circles?

....

8. Do you think implementing circular economies in your business will be a drag on profits? If so, why? Have you done the analysis?

....

CHAPTER 2

THE POWER OF CIRCLES

"There is never a lack of resources, only a lack of resourcefulness."
—TONY ROBBINS

Circles have an inherent power that is transformational. We begin life as babies crawling on the floor, then children toddling from one piece of furniture to the next, until finally, we get our first bike. The turning wheels transport us from where we are to any place we want to go. Suddenly, our view changes. We can go further faster and see more of the world more quickly. We might graduate from a tricycle to a bicycle, and then a motorcycle or car, moving faster and faster with each new set of wheels. All those new experiences change our perspective of just how big the world is—and how small we are in it. Yet, each one of us and how we choose to live our lives has an impact on that world.

Do you remember the first time you rode a two-wheel bicycle—without training wheels? Do you remember the feeling of freedom, exhilaration, of speed—of fear...and of that first crash! I was recently reminded of these emotions when my five year old son took off on his bicycle for the first time. There was magic and mystery in his eyes—not to mention the mischievousness. Since the wheel was discovered around 6000 years ago, virtually all humans have experienced the magic of this amazing circle.

Circles have been symbols of eternity since the beginning of time (excuse the oxymoron)—they have no beginning and no end. In a sense, they are the very definition of sustainability. One can only imagine how amazing it felt to Magellan when he discovered that our planet did not have edges—another amazing sphere.

So if circles are so powerful, why do we focus so much on linear relationships in business?

A supply chain is sustainable if it positively adds value to the three Ps: People, Planet, and Profits. Linear logistics models typically do not do this and thus are not sustainable. The majority of logistics around the world and certainly in Japan are linear based.

We can choose a linear path, moving from one goal to the next without consideration for where our path leads us, or the effect our path has on the world. Or we can seek to understand the effect of our footsteps on each path we take, understanding that for every step there is impact, and that impact ultimately affects our own lives in some way for better or for worse. Unlike the hunter-gatherer cultures of the past, a linear path does not create a circular economy.

Following a linear path produces waste that's unusable, instead of reusable. This waste can be damaging to others and to the environment. A linear path uses precious resources and returns nothing of value.

Contrast this with the practice of following a circular path—one that sees "leftovers" as another resource and takes steps to ensure that the waste created is usable, and not stripped of its value. In fact, it eliminates the concept of "waste" entirely. In a circular path, everything is a resource. If you're holding on to the idea of waste, then you're primed to look for waste in your process.

But if you've made that mindset shift to eradicating waste, then you're simply focusing on using a hundred percent of the resources you have, and nothing is waste. If you do end up generating leftovers meant to be thrown away, then you're immediately looking for a more efficient way to make your product, or to use better resources. A person or company that plans in advance to utilize the resources they have to the fullest extent never runs out of resources. They are resource-full, or resourceful.

An example of the circular skill "Waste-as-a-Resource" (Figure 2.1) demonstrated by our company, SVL, is found in salad production. When salad vegetables are cut up, about 30 percent of the vegetables are deemed "waste" not necessarily because they're unfit for human consumption, but because most people do not want to eat wilted lettuce, cucumber peelings, and pepper stems and seeds. This vegetable waste was traditionally treated as burnable trash, costing a business twenty to thirty cents per kilo for disposal. Our company, viewing the vegetable leftovers not as waste but rather, a resource, installed bio-bins where the vegetable leftovers could be collected. This material was then processed into fertilizer that could then be sold at a profit. This not only saved the cost of burning the material, it prevented the pollution caused by burning while creating a natural source of fertilizer in which more vegetables could flourish.

As another example of our company's commitment to sustainability and how we leverage the power of circles, our nonlinear strategy also includes how we utilize communication. Whenever someone in our business has an interaction with a client, we capture it through a discussion, an email, or a text message. We make sure that every interaction is not only recorded, but also looped back to an action item. We don't allow any interactions to "go to waste." This is a soft skill way of demonstrating the power of circles and sustainability. In logistics, the people who have the most touch points with customers are often the truck drivers. The truck pulls up and the client is there waiting. The driver greets the client and makes small talk, and the client could be having a good day or a bad day. Either way, the client often gives feedback to the driver. It's important to us to capture that feedback, where some companies would probably dismiss it. This takes training, because most drivers tend to be introverts—that's one reason they gravitate toward truck driving in the first place. Since they are often the face of your company, you can capitalize on those contacts and derive more value from your people by capturing their client interactions. We are particular about the drivers we hire. We train them well, and we make sure they understand their role as marketers in the business. Their uniforms must look clean, and they must present a neat, professional appearance. Some of the larger logistics businesses have figured this out, but many companies hire delivery drivers without considering the fact that these people are interacting with customers all day. You can circle the feedback they receive back into the business to improve client relationships.

PRACTICING WHAT WE PREACH

One of the largest mayonnaise and fresh vegetable companies in Japan is one you may be familiar with: Kewpie. In cooperation with Kewpie, we, the authors of this book, set up our regional business as follows. The differences between ours and the traditional, linear model of logistics are extraordinary.

The first thing to note is that our trucks are rarely empty. The vegetables are picked up from the farmers. At any site where byproducts are created, bio-bins are installed to manage the raw "waste." Vegetable byproduct generated at supermarkets and other points of sale is also collected. The material collected in these bio-bins isn't burned; it's transformed into a new, value-added product. Within twenty-four hours, it's reduced to fertilizer and taken to the fields where the vegetables are grown. The resulting vegetables grown from this all-natural, chemical-free fertilizer are stronger, more disease resistant, and have higher nutritional value. We also recycle all of the cardboard used to transport the vegetables.

On the people side, our employees are better compensated than their counterparts at our competitors. We have strict no-harassment policies, and both men and women take parental leave as a matter of policy. As you can imagine, young, intelligent, driven people are eager to work for companies like ours, so we are able to hire the best and the brightest.

This must be costing us a bundle, right? Actually, the opposite is true. Our margins are better than our linear-based competitors.

Production processes often create byproducts that are not waste, though they are often treated as such. Choosing to treat these byproducts as resources is the first step in another circular skill, "Circular Design." Another skill, "IoT and Technology," requires a certain amount of low-level technology, along with logistics, the skill represented by the "Circular Supply Chain." Still another skill, "The Circular R's," refers to "reduce, reuse, and recycle." Our company is always looking for economically feasible ways to enlist these skills and improve profitability in the process. (See Figure 2.1.)

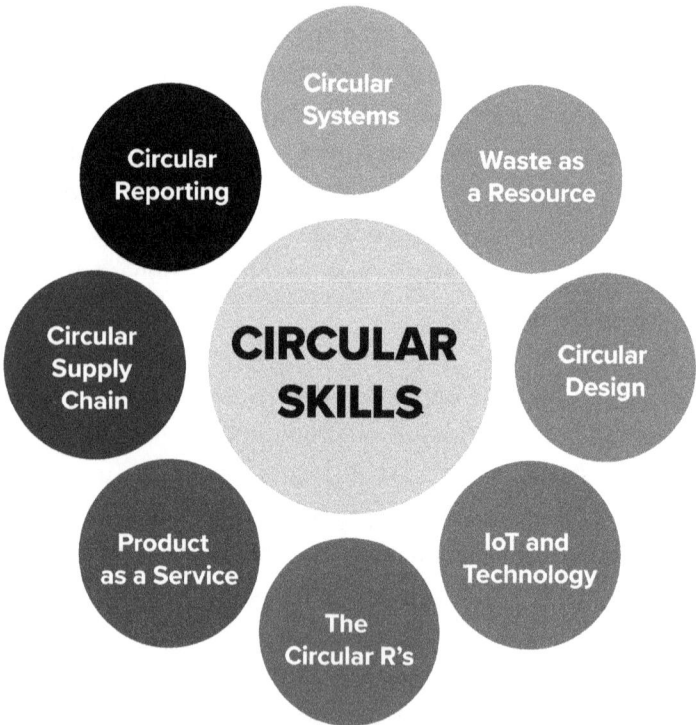

Figure 2.1

A company that ignores the power of circles is destined to operate under an incredible handicap versus their competitors. Instead, leave the linear way of doing business behind. Get ahead of the curve, embrace the power of circles, and see where it takes you. Acknowledge it, harness that power, and capitalize on it. You don't need to reinvent the wheel (which, by the way, are circles). Look for ways to operate where your outputs affect the world in a positive way, and that positive impact affects your inputs in a way that benefits your business.

CIRCLES OVER TIME

Humans have been fascinated by circles for thousands of years, at least since the idea of heliocentrism was introduced. Earth and other planets revolve around the sun in a mostly-circular orbit. The moon too was observed to orbit Earth. Circles were used as reference points in building the Great Pyramids of Giza, and they were put to use to move the great stones in the actual building of these structures.

Circles turn up throughout history: Magellan discovered that the world wasn't flat. Astronomers found that the moon and the planets are orbs, not flat disks. Our galaxy and others have a circular structure. At the atomic level, protons and neutrons revolve in circles around each other. From particles too miniscule to observe with the human eye, to those so astronomical in size that we struggle to comprehend them, circles are everywhere. More recently, we've all seen images of the coronavirus, which is also a circle.

Despite the innate power of circles, businesses have moved away from the early circular approaches to capitalism in lieu of linear patterns. This is primitive thinking. It's like walking to the river to get a bucket of water, using the water to wash your clothes, and throwing the dirty water—along with the laundry detergent—on your lawn. What if you instead filtered the water and used that clean water to grow vegetables to eat? Better yet, what if the laundry detergent was fully biodegradable? That is the kind of circular thinking that's less wasteful and more sustainable. That kind of thinking considers the energy spent on every task and how those tasks can be more impactful.

Instead of limited, primitive thinking, the power of circles is about looking at the whole opportunity. It sees the multiple stages of every process and the effects of each stage on the next, rather than viewing them individually and/or independently (out of context). This sustainable way of doing business is better for people, for the world, and for business.

Consider the water example. What if you had an economical process for cleaning used water and incorporating it into a new product that you could sell? What if you received tax incentives for that practice? What if you advertised this process and attracted a new market of customers to your brand? Think of all the opportunities that are possible with the power of circles, opportunities you could miss out on with linear thinking.

A LINEAR PATH IS A TERMINAL PATH, BUT A CIRCULAR PATH IS FOREVER

A company that continues on a linear path, using resources with no concern for what becomes of people or environments, has a limited future. Just like their linear path, they have a beginning and an end. Focusing on simply getting from one point to the next is linear thinking; its path is, by definition, terminal. Likewise, the business's path is terminal.

On a larger scale, we can compare countries and their resourcefulness. The fewer resources a country has, the more resourceful it must become. Countries with limited resources must learn to maximize those resources and seek to create circular infrastructures where waste—not resources—are limited.

Let's take Japan and Canada, for example. Japan is an island country surrounded by water. Other than fish, there are hardly any natural resources. The Japanese archipelago is a series of volcanic islands, so there is also very little living space. The only reasonably large flat area is the Kantō plain, which is where Tokyo is situated. Otherwise, it is mostly mountains, with just 11.5 percent arable (livable) land, which is located close to the ocean. Comparatively speaking, Japan has very little fresh water, and so it has limited hydroelectricity. There are few trees, and minerals such as gold are scarce. Circular infrastructures in Japan aren't simply the logical solution—they're the only solution.

Now look at Canada, a country with virtually unlimited resources. Canada has the largest number of lakes in the world. In fact, it has more lakes than the rest of the world combined. A large percentage of those lakes have potable water. The country has enormous deposits of natural gas, gold, iron, diamonds, and uranium. It has lots of trees. Its coasts supply water for hydroelectricity and fish for eating. Canada has so many resources, it doesn't even know how much it has.

To someone in Japan, Canada's resources seem unlimited. Yet Japan—with its land mass of 145,914 square miles—supports 126 million people. And it is a relatively wealthy country. Compare that to Canada's land mass of 3.855 million square miles and a population of only 38 million. How does Japan, a tiny resourceless country that's about the size of California, support so many people?

The answer is **resourcefulness**. Despite its lack of resources and the high demand on them due to the population, Japan is extremely productive. Historically Japan, because of its lack of resources, has been forced to forge global relationships with countries that provide resources. The country gets its oil from overseas. For many years, Japan relied on other countries for food such as beef and wheat. While there are many geopolitical reasons for the country's productivity, from the effects of the Second World War to the thousands-year-old culture versus Canada's hundreds of years, the core of their productivity is resourcefulness. Countries like Japan with few resources maximize any resource that they have or are able to get their hands on out of necessity—while countries that have so many, like Canada, underutilize them.

You see the same phenomenon across countries, companies, and even households. Where resources are plenty, they are often wasted, or at the least, used inefficiently. People who have too much tend to become lazy. They use resources with no concern for where they came from or how much is left. They don't pay attention to all the waste they create either, or how they might be sullying the land, or destroying relationships with others. Old wisdom says, "waste not, want not," but few remember it.

Despite their practically unlimited resources, countries like Canada always seem to be in the red financially. How does that happen? Can you imagine if Canada, with all its resources, or the United States for that matter, learned to be as resourceful as Japan? Imagine the potential.

A country without its own resources has to get them from other countries. They might have to buy iron from North America, or iron ore from Australia, and turn that ore into steel. But to compete in the steel market, they have to be more strategic than countries that have iron ore as a natural resource. Those countries can sell steel for a lower price because iron ore is readily available. Countries that purchase iron ore, however, have to add more value or create a high-value product to be competitive at all. Japan, for instance, buys its iron ore and uses its steel to make high-quality cars the world wants. Making better cars is how Japan makes money, and that is being resourceful. This is how it continues to be competitive in the global market.

KEY TAKEAWAY

Being more resourceful makes a country, or a company, more sustainable. That sustainability, born out of necessity, is a time-honored metaphor in countries with few resources. As the world globalizes, it becomes clear that a country or a company that makes the effort to be even marginally more resourceful can be extraordinarily competitive. Businesses that come to that realization can position themselves to win in expanding global markets.

GUIDED REFLECTIONS:

1. What is your company's definition of waste?

   ....

2. How do you evaluate your resources, including human resources?

   ....

3. What does your company dispose of that it could be repurposing as a resource?

   ....

4. What processes within your business are benefitting from the power of circles?

   ....

5. What linear processes does your business have that could benefit from the power of circles?

   ....

CHAPTER 3

ENVIRONMENTAL, SOCIAL, AND CORPORATE GOVERNANCE

"Compassion is the basis of morality."

—ARTHUR SCHOPENHAUER

In 2004, someone in the banking industry got the bright idea of putting together subprime mortgage-backed securities—a variation on mortgage-backed securities that began in the eighteenth century. Mortgage-backed securities are essentially mortgages packaged together and sold as high-yield, high-interest securities. The theory was that whoever packaged and sold the securities would make money, whoever purchased the securities would make money, and more people who wanted to buy homes could become homeowners. A win-win for everyone.

Packaging mortgage loans gave banks and mortgage lenders more capital and they, in turn, had more money to loan people who wanted to buy a home. Banks and other lenders relaxed the rules around who they loaned money to and how much was loaned, requiring less collateral and allowing lower incomes from borrowers. This ultimately led to giving home loans to people who typically wouldn't have qualified for them and allowing people who would qualify to borrow much more.

As the loans turned risker, someone in the banking industry stepped forward with the idea of *subprime* mortgage-backed securities (MBS)—this was the bright idea. All the banks had to do to get rid of the bad loans, also known as subprime mortgages, was package them with a bunch of high-quality loans in a mortgage-backed security. This way, the mortgage-backed security would still be rated very highly. And because banks were becoming less transparent about the contents of these securities, these bad loans would pass unnoticed.

It *was* a great idea—for the banking industry. Banks, investors, ratings companies, and Wall Street in general all made a tremendous amount of money. But it wasn't so great for the rest of the world. What seemed like a good investment was actually a security comprising a bunch of home mortgage loans that the borrowers couldn't afford. They had high ratings when they were actually very low-quality investments. At the same time, the rise in home sales created a housing bubble, driving the price of real estate to unreasonable levels. It was a disaster waiting to happen.

Around the second half of 2007, subprime mortgages began falling apart. It became public knowledge that these subprime mortgage-backed securities weren't worth what investors had been led to believe. Several financial institutions were left holding the bag, so to speak. They were stuck with a great deal of non-performing loans that nobody wanted, so they had no way to acquire equity. Eventually, they had to adjust the values of the loan-backed securities.

Eventually, the values were drastically reduced to a tiny percentage of the selling price. Investors who had purchased the securities lost an incredible amount of money. Mortgage lenders who had doled out subprime loans were financially ruined. This led to the downfall of several Wall Street firms as well as the collapse of the mortgage system and the financial system that supported it. Another, perhaps even more tragic result of the whole mess was what happened to the people who took out these loans. Many of them were locked into adjustable-rate mortgages with initial low interest rates, but after the bubble burst and interest rates rose, these homeowners were stuck in mortgages they couldn't afford. Many ended up in upside-down mortgages, where they owed more on their loans than their properties were worth. Many others, unable to pay their mortgages, lost their homes.

The subprime mortgage crisis was a scandal caused by a lack of corporate governance that had far-reaching impacts on the financial world and on society. In the United States, it contributed to the Great Financial Crisis. It also resulted in the creation of compliance laws to prevent a similar lapse in governance from ever happening again.

Before those laws were put in place, the government lowered interest rates and flooded the market with liquidity in order to rescue banks and other corporations affected by the crisis. Otherwise, these businesses would have had to pay for their capital, exacerbating their financial difficulties. Interest rates were lowered, and the Troubled Asset Relief Program (TARP) was initiated by the US Treasury, where the government lent large amounts of capital to financial institutions to keep them afloat and stabilize the country's economy. The economic crisis wasn't limited to just the US—it had global ramifications. Japan adopted negative interest rates to maintain and sustain the financial system.

You might think that offering negative interest rates would

promote spending, but in fact, quite the opposite is true. In economic downturns, people typically hold onto their money and wait to see some sort of improvement before they ramp up spending again. As a result, deflation can become entrenched in the economy: People stop spending, demand declines, prices for goods and services fall, and people wait for even lower prices before spending. It's a pernicious cycle that can be very hard to break. Negative rates fight deflation by making it more costly to hold onto money, incentivizing spending. Theoretically, negative interest rates would make it less appealing to keep cash in the bank; instead of earning interest on savings, depositors could be charged a holding fee by the bank. Simultaneously, negative interest rates would make it more appealing to borrow money, since it would push loan rates to rock-bottom lows. In Europe and Japan, however, where negative rates emerged, this did not happen. Rather, consumers shopped around for even slightly higher interest rates at banks. Some even opted to lock their hard cash and/or assets into vaults to preserve them for the future as they assumed that inflation would be next.

There were many casualties. Homeowners lost their homes. Some declared bankruptcy. Many had their life's savings invested in those homes, so when they lost that real estate, they lost everything they had earned over their lifetime. The value of real estate tanked.

The subprime mortgage crisis is just one example of the potential for disaster created by a lack of governance, in this case, corporate governance. Environmental impact policies and social impact policies are also critical to maintaining a healthy, sustainable, and financially successful country, corporation, and community.

Environmental, social, and governance (ESG) goals focus on the environmental and societal impact of a business, as well as the governance of that business, to determine the company's future financial performance. The measurement considers both risk and profitability. Though the terminology is relatively new, the concept of ESG investing and ESG corporate strategies has been around for a very long time.

ESG OVER TIME

Today, the acronym ESG is common among owners of capital who are seeking out companies, products, and systems to invest in, based on criteria beyond balance sheets and profit and loss statements. The concept applies to governments as well. At the end of the day, it comes back to investing in your own company. If your company or a company you invest in is destroying the environment, at some point those actions will adversely affect both the top line and the bottom line. Eventually, those practices are not sustainable, leading to the company going out of business.

The term ESG was coined by John Elkington, co-founder of the business consultancy SustainAbility, in 1994. Until that time, many investors weren't very concerned with the environmental impact policies, social impact policies, and corporate governance of the companies in which they invested. This wasn't true of all investors. Smart, forward-thinking investors had already known that the best investments are those that have higher returns and less risk over time. These investors sought out companies to invest in that were transparent about their actions and that showed a lot of long-term promise due to—among other things—sustainable practices around their impacts on the environment and society. Defining the concept of ESG began a conversation that put sustainable practices in the spotlight. Warren Buffet, a key investor, understands the strategy and reasoning behind investing in companies that prioritize sustainability. He said, "In the short-run, the market is a voting machine…but in the long-run, the market is a weighing machine…"[13] Benjamin Graham in *The Intelligent Investor* famously said, "A stock is not just a ticker symbol or an electronic blip; it is an ownership interest in an actual business, with an underlying value that does not depend on its share price."[14]

Until recently, many investors believed that if they directed their investments toward companies that operated more ethically, they would probably have lower returns. Companies that took resources from the environment with no concern for the impact on that environment from which those resources were taken, or the impact of the waste created by production, or for where those products ended up, were believed to have a competitive edge financially, thus more likely to have higher revenues, profits, and in turn, higher returns to the investor.

In fact, Milton Friedman's economic theory, which held considerable sway until 1998, asserted that management should not be concerned with the ethics of their business practices. Their sole aim should be to maximize profits for shareholders, and it was the responsibility of the shareholders to worry about the ethical side of the business. Yet, even in this hard-nosed definition of capitalism, Friedman assumes a basic level of ethics: "There is one and only one social responsibility of business—to use its resources and engage in activities designed to increase its profits so long as it…engages in open and free competition, without deception or fraud."[15]

---

13 Warren E. Buffet to shareholders of Berkshire Hathaway, Inc., Omaha, NE, March 1, 1994, https://www.berkshirehathaway.com/letters/1993.html.

14 Benjamin Graham, *The Intelligent Investor: A Book of Practical Counsel*, rev. ed. (New York: HarperBusiness Essentials, 2006), xiii.

15 H. Jeff Smith, "The Shareholders vs. Stakeholders Debate," *MIT Sloan Management Review*, July 15, 2003, https://sloanreview.mit.edu/article/the-shareholders-vs-stakeholders-debate/#ref2.

Even with the main goal of profit, Friedman assumed that all companies would operate on a basic moral code—no lies, cheating or willful deception—that many unsustainable corporations today are violating. They claim hard-nosed capitalism as their excuse but lies and hypocrisy were never capitalism's way. Friedman's doctrine, which is also known as the shareholder theory, is one way of looking at capitalism. There is another, called the stakeholder theory. Everyone impacted by a company is a stakeholder: the customers, the employees, the management, even the shareholders. In other words, they are "individuals and constituencies that contribute, either voluntarily or involuntarily, to [a company's] wealth-creating capacity and activities, and who are therefore its potential beneficiaries and/or risk bearers."[16]

As H. Jeff Smith writes: "Although there is some debate regarding which stakeholders deserve consideration, a widely accepted interpretation refers to shareholders, customers, employees, suppliers and the local community."[17] Thus, if you shift your focus from shareholders to stakeholders, then you are shifting your focus from only pleasing shareholders to taking care of everybody. This is the essence of stakeholder capitalism or the stakeholder theory.

Notably, as different as they are, both theories share a common, bedrock assumption that successful companies pay attention to environmental impact, social impact, and corporate governance—essentially, ESG strategies. We believe the heart of capitalism is corporations generating outsized profits while adding extraordinary value to society, and that definition incorporates a bit of both shareholder capitalism and stake-

---

16   Smith, "Shareholders vs. Stakeholders Debate."

17   Smith, "Shareholders vs. Stakeholders Debate."

holder capitalism. It's balanced on the meeting point between those two theories, and the path to getting there is through sustainability.

Then in 1998, journalists Robert Levering and Milton Moskowitz compiled a list of the one hundred best companies to work for, first as an article in the magazine *Fortune*, and later, as a book.[18] Among their criteria, the pair considered the best-practicing companies in the United States with regard to their environmental and social impacts, bringing to the forefront the importance of those two factors of ESG goals. Later, Moskowitz noted that corporate governance was also an important aspect of responsible investment.[19]

According to Wharton finance professor Alex Edmans, the one hundred best companies to work for outperformed their peers in terms of stock returns by 2 to 3 percent a year from 1984 to 2009, and they delivered earnings that systematically exceeded analyst expectations.[20] A report from the law firm Freshfields concluded that not only was it permissible for investment companies to integrate ESG issues into investment analysis, but it was arguably part of their fiduciary duty to do so.[21]

Though the traditional definition of a good investment is one that maximizes returns, investment companies also have a

---

18 Brian Ballou, Norman H. Godwin, and Rebecca Toppe Shortridge, "Firm Value and Employee Attitudes on Workplace Quality," *Accounting Horizons* 17, no. 4 (December 2003): 329–341, http://dx.doi.org/10.2308/acch.2003.17.4.329.

19 Alex Edmans, "Does the Stock Market Fully Value Intangibles? Employee Satisfaction and Equity Prices," *Journal of Financial Economics* 101, no. 3 (September 2011): 621–640, https://doi.org/10.1016/j.jfineco.2011.03.021.

20 Edmans, "Does the Stock Market Fully Value Intangibles?"

21 Freshfields Bruckhaus Deringer and UNEP Finance Initiative, *A Legal Framework for the Integration of Environmental, Social and Governance Issues into Institutional Investment*, October 2015, https://www.unepfi.org/fileadmin/documents/freshfields_legal_resp_20051123.pdf.

legal responsibility to invest responsibly and within an sustainable profitability framework. Maximizing returns by investing in companies that are destroying the environment and society is an act against those investment companies' fiduciary duty.

How a company is managed, its governance, also affects a company's risks and returns. All three of these ESG factors play into sustainability. A business that is poorly managed, with little to no transparency, and that operates with little to no regard for its impact on the environment and society, will underperform.

Much has changed in the past thirty years, and ESG has become less a question of philanthropy and more one of practicality. Making business decisions that benefit the world isn't simply a nice thing to do—it's a good investment. It could almost be seen as a secret weapon of capitalism that allows the good corporate citizen, *the savvy capitalist*, to competitively generate outsized profits while adding extraordinary value to society.

A movement that began in the early 2000s challenged the historical assumptions regarding the financial effect of ESG factors. Until the 1990s, the common belief among investors was that ethically responsible companies were less profitable. The *100 Best Companies to Work For* and other publications challenged that idea and, in time, proved it to be false.

ESG AS WE SEE IT TODAY

Today, most investment companies have an ESG division or team, or ESG analysts. When investment managers compile a portfolio of companies to invest in, those portfolios are evaluated on their adherence to ESG criteria and even given an "ESG score." The companies that fall short are excluded from the portfolio. The standards are becoming, and will continue to be tougher, while transparency demand gets higher.

ESG IS *NOT* A POLITICAL LEVER

There is a real and present danger of ESG being used as a political tool to manipulate corporations and individuals towards a specific political goal. This, in fact, will only serve to have the opposite impact of moving further away from capitalism and from greater profitability. Giving in to political pressures or special interests in the name of ESG will almost certainly lead to the destruction of stakeholder value and must be avoided here.

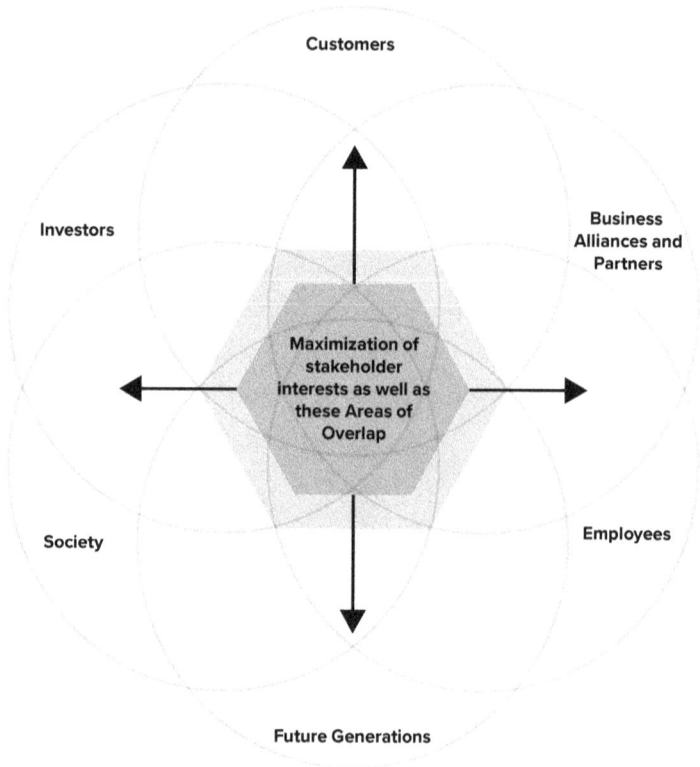

Customers

Investors

Business Alliances and Partners

Maximization of stakeholder interests as well as these Areas of Overlap

Society

Employees

Future Generations

Figure 3.1

Here's how this works. Traditionally, investment companies looked at profitability to determine if a company's share price was overvalued or undervalued. With ESG investing, the parameters have changed. Figure 3.1 gives you a good idea of what investors are looking for when they evaluate a company according to ESG criteria.

Each of these circles represents a stakeholder: customers, business partners, employees, future generations, communities and societies, and investors. A company with good ESG strategies considers its impact on each of these six stakeholders, not just one or two.

When an investment firm evaluates a business according to ESG criteria, they look at data for these six circles. These are the parameters by which they evaluate the true value of a corporation, and they then compare that true value against the company's current share price to determine whether or not the business is a good investment.

For example, say a business has been focusing on short-term profit at the expense of the environment and their employees. This would be an automatic zero valuation for the parameter "future generations." "Communities and society" would also be zero value. "Customers" may be a partial value, depending on what the business is. "Employees," again, will be zero value. That is three circles already at zero value, and one with a partial grade. In all likelihood, an investment firm will determine that this corporation's true value is lower than its current share price and will exclude it from its portfolio. They would look to short-sell or underweight the shares rather than buy them or overweight them.

While ESG investing is certainly a great step, we still have a long way to go. Some of this work is currently no more than window dressing. An investment firm might do some simple analysis to satisfy clients that their money is in an "ESG-compliant investment." We believe that this analysis should be rigorous. Yet, the information can be difficult to uncover. For example, if a company is firing all of their pregnant women to avoid paying maternity leave, and due to an underlying—albeit erroneous—belief that employees without families are more productive, they are not going to publish that fact. So how does one discover a company's true practices before they invest in that company? If that kind of information were readily available, would investors have trusted their clients' money in companies like Enron before the 2001 scandal that took down the whole company? Or in British Petroleum before the Deepwater Horizon oil spill? Or in any company whose goods are produced by children working in factories, usually in unhealthy and even dangerous conditions?

Consider my own experience with Mitsubishi Morgan Stanley. Without the public lawsuit against the company, investors would be unaware of the hypocrisy between the company's outward claims of it being a family-friendly employer and its actual treatment of parents-to-be.

Where do you find this information before you invest? Before it's too late? Worse, with this new focus on ESG, some companies are more careful to hide their negative actions and impacts. Large corporations produce gorgeous brochures filled with meaningless reports. There might be a photo of a beautiful pregnant woman holding a baby, with comments about how the company treats all its employees well through all of their life's events. They might brag about their retention rates, noting how few people leave because their culture and benefits are so excellent. There could be a two-page layout of a lush forest and an article about how the company has made an investment in a national park in Argentina. Meanwhile, they're preventing women from taking leadership roles and pressuring them to return to work soon after giving birth. They're destroying the environment in another South American country. So, while there have been attempts to be more ESG-compliant, the hard work is yet to be accomplished, and in many cases it hasn't even begun.

In fact, to the extent that ESG has led to these types of nefarious and deceptive "virtue signaling" behaviors, it will, unfortunately, have a negative impact on real, value-added transformation. We believe, however, that AI, legitimate research, and sophisticated/transparent data will be the eventual solution to this issue.

For companies new to ESG, tools are available. Research firms such as MSCI, Sustainalytics, and Truvalue Labs offer ratings to investors and corporations based on ESG factors.[22] A company could discover their current score and then work with a consultant to reach a higher score as a corporate goal. At SVL, we found that, although we consult in the logistics business, many of our global clients are looking for guidance on how to become more sustainable overall. We've been able to leverage our diverse background in the public and private sectors to provide that advice, and we continually work with our customers to move together towards these goals.

Returning to the power of circles, we see that businesses that choose a circular approach over a linear way of doing business have a better chance at success not only by ethical standards, but also as profitable enterprises. ESG, at its essence, may be seen as a measure of sustainability. Adhering to the criteria of ethical practices around corporate governance, society, and

---

22 MSCI ESG Research LLC: https://www.msci.com/; Sustainalytics: https://www.sustainalytics.com/; Truevalue Labs, a FactSet Company: https://www.factset.com/.

the environment in a way that considers one's actions beyond that of simply attaining a goal, but rather as having a perpetual effect, leads to a healthier company fit to withstand the rigors of the business environment.

RISKS TO BUSINESSES THAT FAIL TO ADOPT THE PRINCIPLES OF ESG

Scandals like Enron and Deepwater Horizon have brought to light the risks of failing to adopt ESG standards. The conversation about the environment and social justice has become much louder. People aren't just concerned with the short-term effects of nefarious or negligent actions; they worry about the permanent damage to people and to the planet.

Climate change, greenhouse gas emissions, biodiversity, and waste management are common topics of conversation among the world's populations. People worry about a future where natural resources are depleted, about a planet that's no longer able to sustain life. They think about survival on an uninhabitable Earth. This is about more than the future of business—it's about the future of the human race.

If the resources required to manufacture a product disappear or become scarce, the cost prohibits affordable production and a company won't be able to make its products. Likewise, employees' health and welfare are just as critical to the sustainability of a business. Diversity and inclusion affect productivity and profitability. They affect innovation and agility. A business that markets to a diverse customer base, but does not reflect those people in its own staff, is limited in its ability to truly understand its customers. A business that profits without concern for its impact on customers, as seen in the subprime mortgage debacle, is destined for failure.

But make no mistake, diversity and inclusion isn't about quotas or limits. Rather, it's about hiring the best, the brightest, the most qualified people for a given job regardless of race, personal preferences, ethnic origins, gender—regardless of whether the person has graduated from Harvard or Delhi University and, needless to say, regardless of color. If this is the focus, the team will be extraordinarily diverse and mirror the diversity of one's clients.

Predatory lending as a social practice damages society. Animal welfare within the animal agriculture business is another hot topic that's received much attention as of late. Consumers do not want animals to be tortured in the production of their food, clothing, and personal items, such as cosmetics. They also question the effect of such practices on the environment.

Investors are becoming more interested in a business's management practices and, for that reason, they are asking new questions. They want to know how many women and people of color they have in leadership positions. They also want to know whether multiple generations are represented. They want to know whether there are conflicts of interest. Is the CEO also the chairman of the board? What other outside financial interests does that person have that might influence their decisions? Are the token women on the board related to the managers? Is the government pressuring management to violate ESG strategies and blocking any real progress towards sustainability? How do these new concerns affect a company's ability to attract high-quality talent and how will the answers to those questions affect revenue, profitability, and investors?

BENEFITS TO BUSINESSES THAT EMBRACE ESG

Marui is one of the largest department stores in Japan. It started out as a family-owned, family-run business and grew over time, eventually going public. Brick and mortar stores worldwide, and especially in first-world countries, have been through rough times due to the popularity of online retail, and Marui wasn't immune to these challenges. A department store, whether it is Macy's, Saks Fifth Avenue, or Marui has a large real estate footprint and all the overhead that comes with that footprint, so they have to do well to stay in business. Stores like K-Mart and Sears have closed sites as shoppers turn to Amazon and other online retailers for more choices, the convenience of shopping from home, and next-day and—in some cases—same-day delivery.

Consumers in Japan have also changed their shopping habits, gravitating to online businesses. You can imagine, then, what a large department store in Tokyo, paying Tokyo real estate prices, has to do to survive. They need to generate extremely high returns.

In 2005, there was a changing of the guard at Marui, with the president stepping down and another family member, Hiroshi Aoi, stepping into the role. The business, like many retailers, was struggling. This new president wanted to do something different at Marui. He wanted to leave his mark on the company by taking it in a new direction, with a focus on ESG goals. In a letter published to the Marui website in 2016, he writes: "In response to social changes, we have adopted a perspective emphasizing environmental, social, and governance (ESG) concerns and defined realizing the type of sustainability advocated by this perspective as our new goal. Accordingly, we are advancing initiatives to transform our main business into a socially contributing undertaking with eyes to the future."[23] Marui began implementing the three pillars of an ESG strategy in its own unique way.

To make the company more socially responsible, Aoi made dramatic changes to employee policies, emphasizing maternity and paternity leave for new parents, eight-hour workdays instead of the longer shifts some employees had been putting in, and paid holidays. Japan has a lot of holidays, and many companies don't allow employees to take all of them, or even most of them. The new president also introduced strategies for Marui's wider society, its customers. The stores were redesigned to be more LGBTQ- and disability-friendly, and their clothing brands were diversified to cater to a wider range than just the "standard" size popular in fashion. Marui has always offered credit cards to youths as part of its financial inclusion strategy; now the company expanded this scope into a FinTech business, partnering with other FinTech companies to improve financial freedom.

For environmental policies, the new president shifted focus from recycling clothes to reducing resource usage. He improved corporate governance by, among other changes, slashing the number of internal directors from four to two, which facilitated quicker and more in-depth discussions. None of these ESG strategies are static. Marui is constantly improving and looking for ways to stay ahead of the curve.

I was fortunate to see Aoi speak at a seminar and was quite impressed. His changes led to positive results. People wanted to work there, and they wanted to shop there. Marui was outperforming its competitors, and its stock price went up. Due to the company's success, the cost of equity went down, so it required less money for them to do business.

---

23   Hiroshi Aoi, "Message from the President," MARUI GROUP, November 2016: https://www.0101maruigroup.co.jp/en/sustainability/message/.

Many of Marui's ESG strategies created a simple shift in perspective, which, in turn, increased profits. For example, Marui had a shoe-swapping program in place since 2013, which allowed customers to swap shoes they didn't want for ones that they did. Employees noticed that a startling number of customers were swapping shoes they had recently purchased or barely worn. At any other time in Marui's history, this observation may have led to nothing. But because Marui was focused on reducing wasteful purchases by their customers, the employees dug deeper. They discovered that customers bought the shoes because they liked the design—but the shoes were uncomfortable to wear.

This insight led to the creation of the Rakuchin Kirei shoe line, which emphasizes comfort and a proper fit. This line is now the star attraction of Marui's private brands, with 3.5 million shoes sold by 2016. Marui reduced wasteful buying. They sold more shoes that customers would actually wear and at the same time, increased profits.

This is the ripple effect of ESG strategies. They make the world a better place and, in doing so, improve corporate profitability. When the new president began making these changes, people were worried. A wealthy man, Hiroshi Aoi would have survived financially if his plan failed, but the reputation of his family was on the line, along with his pride, and his future as a business leader. Still, he was confident in his decision and, coming from a long line of leadership at the company, he was not only prepared for his new role, but he had also done his homework and could see where his business was headed:

You may ask why we changed our focus from CSR to sustainability. One reason can be found in changing social trends. A trend we are paying particular attention to is the new emphasis on ESG investment. Investors have previously tended to view investments from a short-term perspective, seeing them as a means to make their money work for them. This is especially true in Japan. The emphasis on ESG investment is an important trend as it represents an increase in the desire of investors to endorse good governance and also to value the resolution of environmental and social issues.[24]

You could say that the president was a man of high morals, based on his ethical choices, and that may be true. However, focusing on environment, social, and governance principles wasn't simply the right thing to do, it was his path to success. You might even say his actions were the greedy thing to do. Whatever his motivations, he made Marui more valuable and increased his own wealth. His reputation, pride, and future at the company also benefited from his actions.

In other words, Aoi took Marui back to the original definition of capitalism: a corporation that generates outsized profits while adding extraordinary value to society. He recognized that businesses function in a web, a collection of diverse stakeholders, and sustaining that web will lead to growth and profit: "We realize that the aid of all of our stakeholders will be indispensable in resolving the issues MARUI GROUP faces and in furthering its evolution."[25]

For corporations that have been around for nearly a century or more, adopting ESG goals can be challenging. Leadership has done things one way for generations and aren't always willing to change. Large companies, too, are slower to evolve. Yet Marui, a multinational corporation with roots dating back to

24   Aoi, "Message from the President."

25   Aoi, "Message from the President."

1931, evolved, and the leadership, employees, customers, and investors reaped the benefits.

Environmental, social, and corporate governance (ESG), and the need for transparency and accountability, isn't limited to the corporate world. The policies of a country are equally responsible, if not more so, for adopting ESG standards if the country is to survive over time. Again, there is no room for virtue signaling—just true, sustainable, massive growth initiatives.

KEY TAKEAWAY

ESG investing may seem like a new concept, but it is how smart investors have always vetted opportunities. The highest quality investment firms have always been concerned with these issues. The terminology brought the concept to the forefront for other investors and created a new environment in the world of finance. The need for the terminology "ESG investing" is evidence of the fact that investing, and perhaps capitalism, got a little off track. The term has become a necessary tool for bringing corporations and investors back in line with the heart of capitalism: generating excess returns while adding extraordinary value to society.

The "adding value to society" piece was diminished over the years. ESG puts it back on the balance sheet and brings awareness of its importance to corporate leadership, investors, employees, and customers. It's no longer simply a nice thing to do, but a mandate for any business with expectations of remaining competitive now and in the future. If a business leader or owner wants their company to be a successful and flourishing enterprise over the next generation, they must focus on ESG policies.

GUIDED REFLECTIONS:

1. If you asked your employees, especially your top-level management, about ESG, would they be able to explain it to you?

....

2. What are your competitors doing around ESG that you are not?

....

3. Is ESG a corporate goal? How is it being implemented?

....

4. Are you having trouble attracting talent? Have you seen a rise in the cost of equity? Has your business suffered any scandals? Do you worry when regulators do inspections of your business? Could you track any of these issues to a lack of policy around ESG, and could the problems be mitigated if you made ESG a corporate strategy and a KPI?

....

CHAPTER 4

ENVIRONMENT

"Without environmental sustainability, economic stability and social cohesion cannot be achieved."

—PHIL HARDING

There are innumerable examples of corporate behavior that has had a destructive impact on the environment. Commercial over-fishing, for example, off the east coast of the United States and Canada, has led to a shortage of fish for people who depend on it for their livelihoods. Over-fishing also has a detrimental impact on the food chain.

The global tuna fishing industry is another example where Asian countries, including Japan and China, have depleted the oceans. The demand for sushi has expanded worldwide, and without regulations in place to control how much tuna can be extracted within a time period, so much is removed that it could take generations for the fish to return to their earlier numbers. This demand has also encouraged illegal activities, because the demand and the market are so large, and the industry so profitable. However, how do you control fishing over such a large expanse of ocean?

THE EARTH QUAKES

A specific environmental incident caused by a lack of consideration for environmental policies, social policies, and corporate governance (sustainable profitability goals) was Japan's nuclear disaster.

Japan is an island nation comprising a series of volcanic islands. Many of the country's volcanoes are still active, and those that are dead may yet come back to life. Mount Fuji, for instance, may erupt at any moment—and it's only 100 kilometers away from Tokyo, a megalopolis with a population of some 37 million. There are other dangers, too. The Japanese archipelago is crisscrossed with fault lines, making it one of the most earthquake-prone countries in the world. It has seen one earthquake disaster after another. Along with the quakes come tidal waves and tsunamis that cause more damage.

Even buildings in Japan are constructed on the concept of transience. Japanese accounting laws state that any wooden structure—and virtually all Japanese houses have core wooden structures—is essentially worthless after thirty years. After twenty years, you can depreciate it in full in four years, but after thirty, it's worth nothing. Compare this to the fifty- to sixty-year depreciation scales in the US or Canada. This is because Japan is a country with volatile weather. There is intense rain for six weeks, the humidity shoots up to more than 100 percent, the wood rots, and then floods and mudslides wash these structures away. This affects how construction is even thought of in the country. Why waste money and materials on a house that could survive when it would be considered worthless in the eyes of the law in thirty years anyway? More importantly, can you afford to waste time carefully building a structure that lasts when your home has been flattened by a mudslide and you need a new roof over your head immediately? Construction companies choose cheap materials that wear out quickly, but that allow them to build houses on an accelerated scale. It's all balanced on the notion of transience.

Does this sound like a good foundation on which to build a nuclear power plant? Yet, that's exactly what they did.

In the seventies, Japan was experiencing extraordinary growth due to global policies such as agreements with the US, where that country would buy practically everything Japan produced. Eager to cash in, the Japanese government decided to build a number of nuclear plants, thirty-three total, around Japan to generate energy for manufacturing. These were built on volcanic islands with fault lines running through them, areas known to be prone to earthquakes, tsunamis, typhoons, and landslides. In fact, they were built in populated areas with a history of massive earthquakes. It was just a matter of time before a quake occurred near one of these plants, and in fact, it's likely that we'll see more of them, as nuclear plants still exist in these areas.

On March 11, 2011, an earthquake struck the Tōhoku region in northern Japan. It impacted nuclear power plants, causing a meltdown. The land within more than a thirty-kilometer radius was destroyed, and likely won't be safe for tens of thousands of years. Food grown on that land isn't safe to eat. The majority of the nuclear spill-off was allowed to run into the ocean, which is not only impacting Japan, but the entire world. And now the Japanese government is consciously dumping nuclear waste into the ocean because they've run out of storage space. Most of Japan's nuclear waste is placed in storage tanks—you can see them lined up for acres and acres. This dumping could continue for years.

Think about that. The spill-off from the Fukushima Daiichi nuclear disaster continues, and now there is fresh radiation being released into these waters. It's visible on radiation maps. No one should be eating fish caught in those contaminated waters or eating animals that feed on the fish from those waters. Yet oceangoing fish like tuna and whales, which have fishing industries built around them, will carry this radiation around the world. Technically, there's a barrier that shows where the radiation ends. But would you trust an ocean barrier enough to eat something caught anywhere near the radiation leak?

The Tōhoku earthquake and the resulting Fukushima Daiichi nuclear disaster destroyed land and contaminated the ocean. It killed 18,500 people instantly. One hundred and sixty thousand people had to abandon their homes. After the disaster, the incidence of cancer and other diseases skyrocketed among people in the area. What was the total number of people affected, and who will be affected in the future, by radiation? The total number of people who died—and who will die—due to the lingering harmful effects on their bodies and to the environment is yet to be determined. All of this happened because someone thought it was a good idea to build nuclear power plants on top of volcanoes. Even after the disaster, they still think it's a good idea. Obviously, Japanese politicians and the elite continue to profit from that decision.

There have been many lawsuits over the 2011 Tōhoku earthquake and the tsunami that followed, and there will likely be many more. The whole incident points to corruption among corporations, government, and the legal system. Courts in Japan typically work for corporations and the Japanese government. As ex-Supreme Court judge Hiroshi Segi says, judges in Japan act in "blind subservience to the system."[26] They are not independent. They pretend to be, but at the end of the

26   Hiroshi Segi, *Zetsubo no Saibansho* (Tokyo, Japan: Kodansha Ltd., 2014).

day, the people who were sued for this disaster were let off, basically scot-free. The courts found the management to be "without fault." Is it a coincidence that all the management are *amakudari*—part of the Japanese aristocracy?

Amakudari is a concept unique to Japan. It is a system where the Japanese elite graduate from prestigious universities, like Tokyo University, and join prestigious corporations, like Mitsubishi or Mitsui. There, they rise through the ranks until they reach senior positions. At this point, Mitsubishi or Mitsui transfers them to one of its many cross-shareholding companies to become CEO. Or they are offered top jobs in the government, in key ministries like METI (Ministry of Economy, Trade and Industry), the Ministry of Finance, the Foreign Ministry, etc. It's a golden parachute: the elite are not expected to do anything but let the organization run itself while they take it easy, enjoy life, and wait to retire. *Ama* means "sweet" and *kudari* means "decline": it's a free pass for the elite to ride out the rest of their years in an extraordinarily sweet fashion.

When the Tōhoku earthquake hit, the management at the electric power company was *amakudari*. Running the electric power company is seen as a cushy position, with no responsibilities—nuclear power runs itself, right? The *amakudari* were in charge when the disaster happened, and they made all the wrong decisions. They hid the truth, they didn't shut down the nuclear power plants in time, they abdicated responsibility. And the courts found them not guilty. And so, the people who lived in that area suffered and will continue to suffer. People lost their land, their homes, and their livelihoods. The land that exists is no longer arable. The damage is incalculable, and its effect will be felt for generations.

The Tōhoku disaster is an extreme example of what can go wrong when businesses make decisions without consideration for ESG, and in particular, the environment. Though perhaps not as dramatic, the planet is destroyed in less obvious ways every day by companies that operate in a linear fashion, moving from one goal to the next with no concern for the resources they replete.

Yet, if they choose to, corporations and governments can utilize resources without damaging the environment. They can find ways to add value to the world while being extraordinarily profitable. In the short term, they will have fewer problems with regulators and may be eligible for government subsidies and tax breaks. They'll find it easier to attract and retain employees and customers. In the long term, these companies will be more competitive and sustainable as they find easier and cheaper access to capital.

EPS AND THE ENVIRONMENT

Expanded Polystyrene or Styrofoam as it is commonly known, is still widely used in supply chains in Japan. This is despite the very common knowledge that it is a carcinogen, it is non-biodegradable, it is largely not recycled resulting in environmental damage, and, in fact, is said to be found internally in about 40 percent of the human population. At our company, Smart Vision Logistics, we are leveraging new technologies in these areas and have decided to take EPS or Styrofoam out of our supply chains, thereby increasing the sustainability of the supply chains. We have done global research and have found biodegradable substitutes and options to fully recycle EPS, and we are currently moving forward with domestic production.

But these are just two simple examples and honestly, we have a long way to go. Most waste in Japan is simply burnt. Most used cooking oil and lard in Japan is not used for biodiesel and is very difficult to dispose of ecologically. (Note: McDonalds Japan largely still uses lard for frying their products. McDonalds globally has almost entirely shifted away from lard to using vegetable oil.) Despite the burden placed on consumers in Japan, the majority of the trash is simply burnt. And this is not sustainable.

THE ENVIRONMENT AND BUSINESS OVER TIME

When it comes to the environment, companies have gotten off track along the way. Instead of being mindful of the impact of their actions on the environment, they have profited from destroying it.

You might remember when fast-food restaurants served just about everything in Styrofoam or EPS foam, which is extremely difficult to recycle. Burning EPS foam releases pollutants into the air, and it's estimated that the material, buried in a landfill, can take hundreds of years to break down.[27] But EPS foam was cheap and convenient. Lower costs meant more profits for business and investors, and besides, customers appreciated the convenience of ESP foam containers. No one was thinking about where all that EPS foam was going once its contents were used up. They'd finish their burger, toss the container in the trash—or worse, out their car window—and forget about it.

Companies that were aware of the environmental damage they were causing weren't broadcasting that fact to anyone.

---

27 Styrofoam is a common word now, but it was originally the name of a brand that used Expanded Polystyrene (EPS) foam for thermal insulation. When we use "Styrofoam" in general context today, we actually mean "EPS foam," which is a closed-cell insulation that is relatively rigid and lightweight.

They kept it quiet, enjoyed their profits, and since investors and customers weren't asking, they saw no need to volunteer any information. If everyone else was turning a blind eye, why should they care? They certainly weren't going to put it in their glossy CSR pamphlets. And while EPS foam is no longer as prevalent in the fast-food industry, other items like individual coffee pods, which can't be recycled without manually separating the parts, continue to flood the market. In the past, consumers may have claimed ignorance but these days, the impact of single-use plastics on the environment is common knowledge.

Today's consumer, however, has become, for the most part, more selective about the companies they buy from, and a company's environmental record can impact buying decisions. At the same time, both consumers and companies have had to rethink not only the environmental cost, but also the financial cost they pay for the convenience of products that cannot be reused, reduced, or recycled. Why buy plastic bottle after bottle of water when you can invest in a refillable container and a water filter? Why contribute to the creation of products and byproducts that contaminate the environment and cost money to manage? There has to be a smarter, cleaner, and more financially and environmentally responsible way to do business.

The information age, technology, the internet, and social media have also made the results of consumers' and companies' actions more visible. It may be difficult to imagine thousands of plastic bottles floating in the ocean, but when photos of floating "islands" of plastic go viral and millions of people see them, the problem cannot be disputed or ignored.

When I was living in New York City, there was no recycling. Everything went into the garbage chute. From there, it went into a dumpster, then a garbage truck, and it all ended up in a landfill far from the city. New Yorkers can now have their recyclable waste picked up beside their trash. More and more people are composting their trash too, in backyards and gardens.

Reuse, reduce, recycle has become the battle cry for getting the garbage problem under control. The planet is literally running out of places to put trash, or anything that can't be recycled. Just a few years ago, China made the decision to stop accepting other countries' trash. Enormous barges packed with plastic and other garbage were left rotting on docks, because China turned them away. That decision forced change throughout the world, as countries were left to find other solutions for managing their waste, and ultimately concluded that they had to stop creating so much of it or recycle or burn it on their own shores.

At the time, Japan wasn't recycling cardboard at all. They were shipping it all to China for recycling. When your waste is burned in another country, it doesn't affect your "green" rankings because you don't include it in the numbers you submit to the UN. In a sense, you are window dressing your numbers and thus are guilty of virtue signaling or, more simply, deception. When Japan had the agreement with China, shipping the cardboard was cheaper than recycling it. This showed that the price of cardboard wasn't properly set—it should have cost more—and also showed that government regulators and corporations weren't thinking about cardboard as a limited natural resource. If you use up all the trees to make cardboard and don't recycle it into new cardboard, you will eventually run out. Everyone was ignoring the incredible value they were giving away; in fact, they were *paying* to have it taken away. Imagine paying $200 to someone to burn your $100 bill, simply because you thought it was dirty or creased around the edges. Ridiculous, right? But that is what this amounted to.

There really should be no trash. Everything is a product. When you're done using something, it shouldn't automatically become trash to be thrown away. Everything can be reused or recycled. Here, our language creates psychological barriers that need to be torn down. Why do we say "trash bag," "wastepaper bin," or "garbage room?" Why are these our default words? If we call them recycling bags, bins, or rooms, then what is in them becomes a new product with potential. It is no longer trash. Changing our language transforms our way of thinking.

With my team, I refer to these materials as "excess resources." For example, a banana peel is not trash/waste, it is simply in excess of what we wanted/required. In effect, we are over-resourced which is a wonderful and profitable situation to be faced with.

Japan experienced this when new policies renamed types of trash as *moppara butsu*, which loosely means "random products." For a long time, the only system of waste disposal in Japan was burning. Since they considered trash as "dirty," trucks that delivered food could not collect trash. This created two linear systems: a truck would deliver the buns and meat to a fast-food restaurant and go back empty, then another truck would come to pick up the trash and take it to be burned.

When recycling became popular, people noticed that certain types of trash were useful. Barely used cardboard, for instance, was being dumped alongside food waste and burned indiscriminately. So Japan created new policies that renamed cardboard and similar items as *moppara butsu* (recyclables). Since they were no longer trash, they could now be transported in the same trucks that carried the food. Two linear systems became one cyclical system: a single truck drove in with the meat and buns and left with the *moppara butsu* for recycling.

A NEW CLASS OF WASTE

In Japan, general waste is known as Ippan Haikibutsu (or in Japanese一般廃棄物). The whole process of general waste management is licensed and regulated. A special license is required to haul general waste. The locations where it is deposited must also be licensed. This dissuaded businesses from hauling materials such as cardboard to recycling centers.

To encourage recycling, a new category was created called *moppara butsu.* This type of waste is recyclable, and businesses can manage it differently. This distinction and exception from the rules of general waste management allows businesses to more easily transport and process cardboard and other recyclable materials.

All it takes to implement this change is a reporting process. Management signs a form that says, "these items are not trash, but *moppara butsu,*" a government official stamps it, and *voila!* You're free to implement a cyclical system. Yet so many companies in Japan don't do this. They still burn their waste.

Making simple changes can have a huge impact on a company. A popular fast-food chain in Japan had a "garbage room" at every location. All the leftover food, paper goods, and containers were piled up in that room. In Japan, a license is required to pick up garbage, but virtually anyone can pick up recycling or excess resources. This restaurant was putting all their cardboard boxes in the garbage room, but decided it was more economical to recycle the cardboard and have it picked up for free. So they changed the name of the room from "garbage room" to "recycling room." It was a small thing, but it was a huge change for the company. They didn't have to pay to have their cardboard picked up by licensed garbage collectors anymore, and their cardboard was recycled for reuse.

Another fast-food chain made another important change. They give out small plastic toys with their children's meals, but they found that the kids usually played with the toys for only a short time, while they were eating. Then they threw them away. They weren't taking them home. Even small plastic toys are environmental pollutants, and this company was producing 1.5 billion of them per year across its global franchises. At the cost of $0.60 per toy, that is $900 million in annual costs. Can you imagine the cost to the environment? They solved this problem by placing recycling bins in their restaurants where kids could toss their toys after playing with them. The toys are recycled into food trays for the restaurant chain, and they're a different color than the normal trays, so you know if you're getting a recycled toy tray.

This was a simple solution that reduces the restaurant's carbon footprint. The toys were "excess resources" and these were re-fashioned into food trays. This also dramatically improved their brand image, and meant that regulators and politicians looked more favorably on them. It's the right thing to do for the environment.

Industry has long been taking a linear approach to business operations. It uses up resources and sends the waste to be incinerated, contaminating the air, and to landfills, contaminating the land. Their trash disappeared from sight, but it wasn't truly gone.

This is a convenient "out" for those who pollute—out of sight, out of mind. Yet, CO_2 produced by burning trash pollutes the air we breathe, and plastic bottles clog our oceans. And all of it is affecting the planet and its inhabitants, including humans.

Yet restaurants in Japan gained a new, nonlinear perspective that is also economical. They came to understand the power of circles in the lifecycle of cardboard and plastic. There is no beginning and no end from the perspective of reuse and recycle. One person's trash can literally be someone else's treasure. For the restaurant, it can also be a new source of revenue as they reimagine trash as excess resources.

Restaurants looking to become more profitable while benefiting the environment have discovered other products that were formerly considered waste. Frying machines use cooking oil that can be used only so many times. Food particles get in the oil, and it has to be replaced with clean cooking oil. Some restaurants now have that used oil treated and turned into biodiesel that's used to transport products to the restaurant. The same oil that's used to cook your French fries is powering the trucks that brought the oil to the restaurant in the first place. Instead of a linear lifetime, the oil follows a circular path, and what was once considered garbage is now a resource.

Running trucks on biodiesel doesn't entirely remove the detrimental impact of CO_2 to the environment but it reduces it. The oil isn't thrown into a landfill or into the ocean. It isn't used as chicken feed, resulting in carcinogenic eggs and poultry. And the more biodiesel that's used, the less crude oil is needed that would have to be removed from the ground. The cost savings to the company is an added benefit, and a motivator for more companies to look at similar approaches to managing their own waste. And as we approach equilibrium in cost with electric or other solutions, the future shall become brighter still. The first movers will have a huge advantage as capital costs drop with ESG investing and a focus on SDGs.

RISKS AND BENEFITS: BECOMING ENVIRONMENTALLY FRIENDLY

The world's population is growing rapidly, and new businesses are started every day. Exploration and technology open up new resources, and globalization provides new markets. Consumerism creates increasingly more and more waste and more impact, and that impact can be good or bad, depending on how those resources are managed.

So what risks or benefits do companies face when deciding how to deal with waste and environmental impact?

The move toward ESG standards and the information age have exposed companies that pollute. Scientists estimate that from the mid-1700s onwards, we've released 2 trillion metric tons of greenhouse gases into the atmosphere, and we're adding 50 billion metric tons to this each year.[28] Savvy investors scrutinize companies at a minute level in terms of their impact on the environment and their carbon footprint. In fact, CO_2 is now a traded commodity that's bought and sold on a market. Being a polluter isn't free anymore—it's costing businesses money and making them less attractive to investors, raising their cost of equity and cost of capital.

In the CO_2 market, a net negative-CO_2 producer sells their negative credits into the market, which is another revenue stream for that business. Companies that are net positive have to buy credits in order to legally advertise that they're carbon neutral. So, if a company's fancy brochure claims CO_2 net neutrality, they may in fact have simply purchased enough credits to make that claim, all the while continuing to pollute the environment. Still, they are paying to make that claim. Their argument

28 Brad Smith, "Microsoft Will Be Carbon Negative by 2030," *Official Microsoft Blog*, Microsoft, January 16, 2020, https://blogs.microsoft.com/blog/2020/01/16/microsoft-will-be-carbon-negative-by-2030/.

for what is essentially lying to the public is that, even though they are CO_2 positive, they're supporting businesses that are CO_2 negative with their credit purchases. Still, there are companies that are sincere about making a difference. Microsoft, for example, is not content with being CO_2 negative, but plans to erase its entire historic carbon footprint. It has pledged that, "By 2030, Microsoft will be carbon negative, and by 2050, Microsoft will remove from the environment all the carbon the company has emitted either directly or by electrical consumption since it was founded in 1975."[29] In other words, it plans to become a CO_2-neutral company since its establishment—an incredible example more companies should follow. Decisions like this change the world, and for the better. Microsoft's goal means it must be significantly CO_2 negative for several years to erase the effects of its past activities. Along with a detailed plan to achieve this, the company has dedicated $1 billion in a climate change innovation fund to develop technologies that can help reduce or remove carbon emissions.

Some corporations are being forced down the path of change by their shareholders. ExxonMobil was recently locked in a battle with its investors about whether or not to include climate advocates on their board of directors. Management was of the strong opinion that these people would not be good for profits, but the investors believed ExxonMobil's climate impact couldn't be separated from its financial growth. Management lost the vote, and two climate experts now sit on the board of directors of this oil and gas giant. Danielle Fugere, president of As You Sow (the shareholder's advocacy group) called this a "watershed moment." She said: "The speed of change is building, and I think we all can acknowledge now that there's

---

29   Smith, "Microsoft Will Be Carbon Negative."

no longer room for these companies to make changes on the margins. They have to jump in and start transitioning to a net zero world."[30]

Adding a number of activists to a board of directors is not the generally accepted solution for a corporate leader seeking to develop environmentally and technologically reliable practices. However, we must find a way to be sustainable. In the case of Exxon, the company's earlier poor decisions put them in a position where they had few options. If they had listened to climate experts in the first place, they likely would not have been pressured to include them in their leadership.

Chevron faced a similar reckoning when 48 percent of its shareholders demanded greater transparency around the company's climate impact. It's not just ExxonMobil and Chevron. This is a trend we're seeing across major oil and gas companies. And it's not just oil and gas—this is happening across industries in a push towards ESG strategies and making businesses more sustainable.

Increasingly, CO_2-positive companies are waking up to a world that's leaving them behind. More and more of them are looking at whether it makes good business sense for them to continue with their current methods and technologies. Some are turning to new ways that lessen their impact on the environment, save them money, and potentially create a new source of revenue—their own credits to sell on the market.

The cost to companies isn't trivial. Aside from buying credits, their cost of equity increases as investors look elsewhere for environmentally friendly investments. Consumers who are

---

30 Akiko Fujita, "Exxon Mobil Shareholder Vote a Watershed Moment for Climate Change," Yahoo Finance, May 26, 2021, https://finance.yahoo.com/news/exxon-mobil-shareholder-vote-a-watershed-moment-for-climate-change-205909507.html.

aware of their practices will shop the competition, companies that aren't damaging the environment or are, ideally, benefitting it. New talent will be harder to attract and will cost more too, because employees want to know that they're contributing to a common good.

The ramifications are manifold. Corporations have the potential to improve their financial stability and may benefit from tax credits. Their brand benefits too, improving their marketing capabilities. Their stock price could increase if more investors see their company as a good investment with a sustainable payoff. They could pay less for hiring and maintaining employees who want to work for their company.

KEY TAKEAWAY

Unless companies are willing to institute their own corporate governance for positive change, they will face increased government regulation, which could hinder their ability to come up with solutions that benefit the environment and their profitability. Already, the scrutiny from the government, consumers, employees, investors, and the general public is on the rise, and there is no reason for it to lessen.

Companies that used to hide their abuses are at higher risk of being found out and having to deal with the legal issues and damage to their brand. A cover-up also shows a lack of respect for ethical corporate governance, fostering a lack of trust among everyone involved.

From a personal perspective, choosing a positive outcome for the environment is surely more in line with a business leader's own values. Or should be. As Warren Bennis said: "Managers are people who do things right, and leaders are people who do the right things." This difference cannot be emphasized enough. Those leaders who choose to make a better world will no doubt feel better about the planet they're leaving to future generations, including their own children and grandchildren. If they don't do it for the financial or business benefits, or the environment, or to satisfy their own moral compass, perhaps their consciences will guide them to make the right decisions for those people whom they care about the most.

When he was leader of the occupation of Japan after the Second World War, General MacArthur faced great resistance to change and general inertia among Japanese society. He famously said, "If you don't like change, you are going to like irrelevance even less." These words hold true today. Change is at the heart of sustainability, and the modern rate of change is always accelerating. Leaders must keep up. Those who are willing to embrace change, to take to heart General MacArthur's words—they will be the ones building the sustainable organizations of today, and they will be our leaders of tomorrow.

GUIDED REFLECTIONS:

1. Do you, as an employee, manager, or leader of your company, understand the impact your company is having on the environment and society?

....

2. Is your overall process as a company contributing positively or negatively to the environment? How?

....

3. What is your definition of "trash" and has it changed over time?

....

4. After reading this chapter and reflecting on your business, has your definition of "trash" changed? Why or why not?

....

5. Can you think of a way for your company to add value to the environment and improve your profitability at the same time?

....

6. When you think about your overall environmental impact as an organization, do you also include the environmental impact of your customers and the other businesses you deal with? Why or why not?

....

CHAPTER 5

SOCIETY AND THE FAMILY

"Family is not an important thing. It is everything."

—MICHAEL J. FOX

"A man should never neglect his family for business."

—WALT DISNEY

M y father died before I was born. Growing up in Canada with a single mom and one brother, from a very young age I dreamed of becoming a father. After moving to Japan the second time and moving up in the financial world, I was excited to be in a place where I felt secure enough to realize that dream.

I was a senior manager at Mitsubishi Morgan Stanley. The Great Financial Crisis that began in late 2007 had led to the downfall of Bear Stearns and Lehman Brothers, and my employer Morgan Stanley was nearing bankruptcy. Investors weren't interested in the company.

That's when the Japanese company Mitsubishi stepped in to save Morgan Stanley in exchange for up to 21 percent of the company, and Morgan Stanley sold Mitsubishi an equity stake worth $9 billion. The story of how it happened is remarkable, and Andrew Ross Sorkin brings to life the tension and uncertainty of the bailout in *Too Big to Fail*. As Sorkin writes, Mitsubishi had expressed a desire to buy a stake in Morgan Stanley, but they delayed closing the deal. They delayed and delayed until rumors began circulating in the market that the deal wouldn't go through. Morgan Stanley's stock continued to fall, closing one day at "$9.68—its lowest level since 1996."[31] Everyone knew what it would mean for Morgan Stanley if Mitsubishi withdrew the deal—bankruptcy.

But there was nothing to do but wait. Mitsubishi said it had every intention of honoring the agreement, but then why weren't they closing the deal? When Morgan Stanley finally got the call from Japan, they were certain Mitsubishi's bankers were on the phone to deliver the bad news. To their surprise, Mitsubishi reaffirmed their intention to buy a stake in Morgan Stanley—but they wanted better terms. Preferred stock instead of common stock.

In hindsight, Mitsubishi did what any company holding all the cards would do. They waited until Morgan Stanley's desperation was high, and then they renegotiated for better terms. There were further complications. Mitsubishi had apparently reached out to the United States government for assurances that it wouldn't buy a stake in Morgan Stanley, thus negatively affecting Mitsubishi's shareholder status. Morgan Stanley, panicked, wrote a letter to the Japanese government to assure them that any involvement from the United States government wouldn't adversely affect them any more than it would affect other shareholders. It seemed like the deal would never close. But finally,

---

31 Andrew Ross Sorkin, *Too Big to Fail: The Inside Story of How Wall Street and Washington Fought to Save the Financial System—and Themselves* (New York: Viking, 2009), 511.

terms were settled, and the contract was agreed. Still, for it to be signed, sealed, and delivered, money needed to change hands.

By this time, Morgan Stanley was on the verge of bankruptcy—balancing on the knife edge. They needed to close this deal by Monday, or their firm would be gone. But Monday was Columbus Day, a national holiday. That means banks were closed and no money could be wired into accounts. How were they going to do this?

Enter Paul J. Taubman, an M&A banker at Morgan Stanley. According to Sorkin in his book, *Too Big to Fail*, "Taubman had a thought: 'They could write us a check,' he said. Taubman had never heard of anyone writing a $9 billion check, but, he imagined, given the state of the world, anything was possible."[32]

And so that's how a $9 billion check came to be. Mitsubishi's representatives flew around the world to the United States on Columbus Day to complete the transaction.

Nakajima opened an envelope and presented Kindler with a check. There it was: "Pay Against this Check to the order of Morgan Stanley, $9,000,000,000.00." Kindler held it in his hands, somewhat in disbelief, clutching what had to be the largest amount of money a single individual had ever physically touched. Morgan Stanley, he knew, had just been saved.

Some of the Japanese started snapping pictures, trying their best to capture the eye-popping amount on the check.

"This is an honor and a great sign of your faith and confidence in America and Morgan Stanley," Kindler said, trying to play the

---

32 Sorkin, *Too Big to Fail*, 513.

role of statesman in his disheveled state. "It's going to be a great investment."

As the Japanese group turned to leave, Kindler, grinning from ear to ear, tapped out a BlackBerry message to the entire Morgan Stanley management team at exactly 7:53 a.m.

The subject line: "We Have The Check!!!!!!"

The body of the message was just two words:

"It's Closed!!!!!!!!"[33]

You can sense the elation in that last message, the knowledge that Morgan Stanley was finally saved. You can also see the ridiculousness of it—a billion-dollar company so crippled they had to close a deal on a national holiday or else they would be annihilated. When we talk about the strange new structure Mitsubishi and Morgan Stanley created post-merger, or when we describe how Mitsubishi Morgan Stanley treated its employees and me, keep the story of this check in mind. Because this is where the company comes from—from that absolute fear of dissolution and a fear that they would have no future at all. It doesn't excuse the way the company's leadership has behaved since that day, but—as we will see—it does explain the culture that has fostered that kind of leadership.

---

33 Sorkin, *Too Big to Fail*, 518.

EVILS BEGETS EVIL

In many ways, the story of this check is also a story of how bad business practices perpetuate other bad business practices. The Great Financial Crisis was itself a very strange phenomenon, fueled by lies and cheating and greed, and there was definitely a regulatory problem. There must have been deep nefariousness in the rating agencies leading up to the crisis. Who was lining their pockets so that they would look the other way? And who was watching the rating agencies themselves? It just proves that if you allow one area of your economy to act in an unsustainable manner, then it quickly leads to other unsustainable behaviors. In 2008, that snowballed into the Great Financial Crisis that ended companies like Lehman Brothers and brought companies like Morgan Stanley to their knees. It's a death spiral, and it only leads to pain.

Pre-merger, Morgan Stanley and Mitsubishi operated as two independent financial organizations in Japan. Post-merger, the companies restructured the business, combining the firms into one holding company called Mitsubishi UFJ Morgan Stanley Holdings. Under the holding company, the two companies were called Morgan Stanley Mitsubishi UFJ and Mitsubishi UFJ Morgan Stanley. If you're confused by the names, you're not alone. The confusion wasn't limited to the naming conventions; it spread throughout the business, and the restructure was not sustainable. But hang in there—I, Glen, will try to explain what happened next as clearly as I can and without adding more confusion.

Changing the company names and combining them under Mitsubishi UFJ Morgan Stanley Holdings seemed like a good idea initially, until they realized that the domestic business was much less profitable, and most of the profits were going to Morgan Stanley Mitsubishi, which handled the global business. Mitsubishi had spent all this money acquiring a stake in Morgan

Stanley, but what they had done with this new restructure was essentially cripple their own local financial securities company in Japan—i.e. Mitsubishi Morgan Stanley—by handing the profitable part of the business to Morgan Stanley Mitsubishi.

That's when Mitsubishi Morgan Stanley hired me. My primary directive was to rebuild their global business to increase profits. In essence, I would be competing with, and taking back business from their partner company, Morgan Stanley Mitsubishi. In 2011, I was excited for the opportunity. I had expertise in building teams and in global business. I jumped in with both feet and brought the division out of the red and into the black very quickly. In a very short time, I grew the business substantially, and the company recognized my work with high evaluations. Everything was going well.

In 2015, I received the best news of all: I was going to be a father. My partner was to give birth overseas, so I had to sort out the details of how we would be together. Because I'm a Canadian, I spoke with the Canadian embassy about getting a passport for my son and found out the process could take some time. The process might take about four weeks, so I approached my leadership with a request for time off.

In Japan, under the Equal Employment Opportunity Law, employers are required to offer pregnant women shorter work hours or flexible work schedules. They can't demote or fire pregnant women, and they are required to provide them with maternity leave. Likewise, under the law, men must be granted up to one year of paternity leave (with even a possibility of extension). During this time, the company is not required to pay him a salary, but the government pays a portion of it. Mothers and fathers must be given the opportunity to return to their jobs without being demoted or fired. These protections are guaranteed under law for adoption cases also.

The law was established to "encourage" companies to stop firing pregnant women. This was the only way to ensure working parents could have children at all, and that more fathers could help with the house and family. It's a great law—on paper. Unfortunately, however, this is not how it works in practice. Japanese companies regularly use scare tactics to discourage parents from taking time off. In fact, maternity leave has effectively slowed or stalled the upward career movement of women who choose to have children. Women who become pregnant are typically sidelined or forced out. Men are simply harassed or fired. Very few corporations follow the law, and fewer government bodies support and enforce it. At the time that my paternity case against Morgan Stanley and Mitsubishi began in 2016, Japan's Ministry of Health, Labor and Welfare estimated that roughly 3 percent of men took paternity leave. The late Prime Minister Shinzo Abe was publicly encouraging men to take a more active role in raising children. We are starting to see how this plays out in the real world. (See Figure 5.2.)

Laws and rules that support maternity and paternity are good for society, and should be appreciated by everyone, including employers. They allow parents to have careers, instead of being made to choose one or the other. Without paternity and maternity leave, potential parents are forced to choose between sacrificing their careers and future earnings or sacrificing the basic human need for family. Ironically, bringing a new life into a family is when wage earners feel most vulnerable, knowing that a baby will increase their expenses. If there is ever a time for parents to need financial security, it's when they're having a baby.

Though paternity and maternity leave is the law in Japan, it's not the reality because corporations don't always honor those laws. As a result, Japan has a demographic problem, as highlighted in Figure 5.1. Thirty percent of the country's population is over sixty-five years old. Every year, fewer and fewer babies are being born. As of 2023, the number of babies born in Japan totaled 758,631, according to the latest health ministry report. This is another record low number representing just half the 1.5 million births recorded in 1983. Frighteningly, this is the eighth straight year of record lows; an incredible 5.1 percent decline from the previous year.

**JAPAN BIRTH RATES PLUNGE TO RECORD LOWS
AS POPULATION CRISIS DEEPENS
(CURRENTLY LOWEST IN RECORDED HISTORY)**

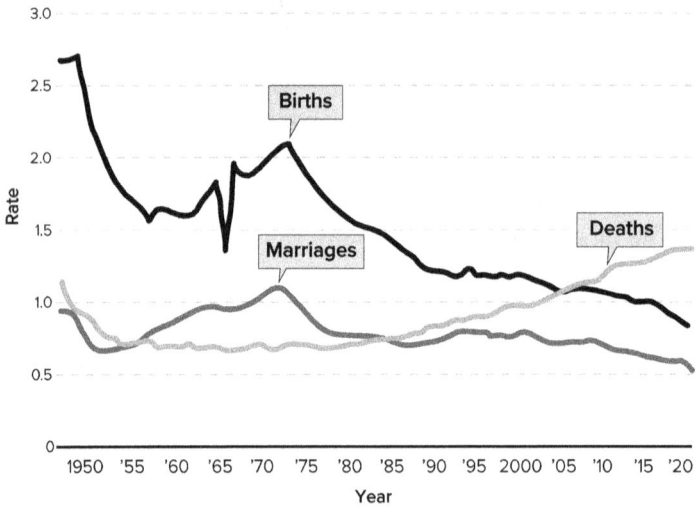

Figure 5.1

If this trend continues, the Japanese population, which is currently about 130 million, could be reduced by half within three decades. Companies' unwillingness to comply with paternity and maternity laws isn't the sole reason for this decline—there are other factors at play. **But when an adult is faced with the distinct possibility of losing their job if they have a child, they will be very hesitant to start a family. Having a child means your costs double, and if your partner is going to lose their job because they had the child, then your income halves.** It's just not a feasible option in one of the most expensive places in the world.

As I mentioned briefly in the introduction, when I asked my leadership for time off, the immediate response from the human resources department was a firm "no." I was confused as to why they wouldn't allow me the time off, so I did some research, and learned that even though it's the law in Japan, few men take it. In fact, in 2015 just 2 percent of men in Japan were taking paternity leave. The reality was that if a man takes that time, he will be demoted or fired. This has changed for the better since 2015, and I've been told that broadly telling my story is responsible for the uptick in men taking leave. As my experiences have become globally renowned, I am often referred to as "the Father" of Japan. Figure 5.2 illustrates the milestones of paternity rates as of 2022.

PATERNITY LEAVE NUMBERS SKYROCKET AS MILLIONS SUPPORT GLEN—"GLEN'S LAW" ENACTED

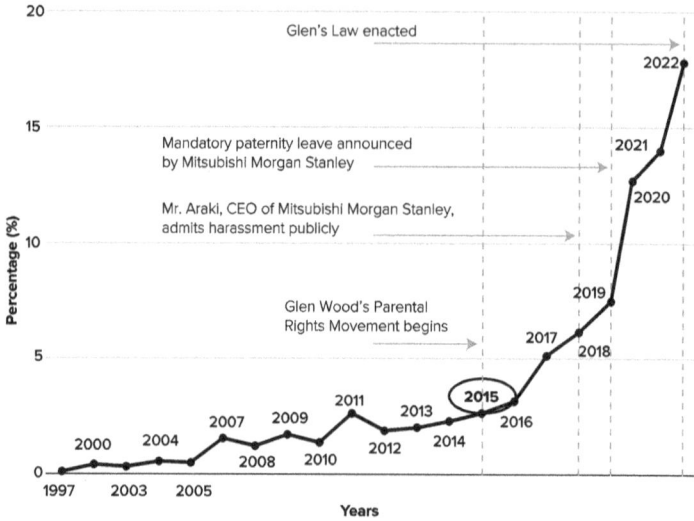

Figure 5.2

MILESTONES

2015 August

- Mitsubishi Morgan Stanley denies Glen Wood's parental leave application.
- In this life-or-death moment, Glen Wood decides to save his son.
- The public battle ensues.

2018 July

- Mr. Saburo Araki, CEO of Mitsubishi Morgan Stanley, makes a global announcement to the media that the company is facing a major issue with harassment and that he will do whatever it takes to eradicate the problem.
- Glen's public court case and global media attention regarding harassment and denial of parental rights is in full swing. Millions lend support.

April 2019

- As Mitsubishi and Morgan Stanley move to fire Glen for taking parental leave, Mitsubishi group tells the media they have made it "mandatory" for all new fathers to take at least one month of parental leave. This continues to impact thousands of employees annually to this day.

April 2022

- So-called Glen's Law (Japanese Parental Leave Law changed on the back of Glen's case against Mitsubishi Morgan Stanley) enacted April 2022: "All employees both men and women must be informed about their right to take Parental Leave." Glen would automatically win his case under this law.

I spoke with a lawyer about my situation and learned that not only was my employer discriminating against me by not notifying me of my legal right to paternity leave and sharing the application with me, but they were also harassing me by rejecting my application. Every time I submitted the request, it was rejected.

I realized my hands were tied. The baby was due on December 5, but while I was trying to figure out how I would handle the passport issue and my rejected paternity leave request, I had word from the hospital. My son was born six weeks early. They didn't think he was going to make it and were sending me photos to show me how tiny he was. He was in the neonatal intensive care unit (NICU), and they wanted me to come right away. I was getting emails and phone calls from the hospital's administration, so I went back to my leadership and told them that I had no choice, I had to go to my family.

Their response shocked me. "Don't worry about it," I was told. "Medicine is so advanced these days, so just go back to your desk and do your job."

My first instinct was to walk out and go straight to the airport, but instead, I stayed for three days, trying to negotiate with the company and to honor my superiors in accordance with Japanese traditions. Those were excruciating days. I was trying to work and talk to my leadership and HR about time off, all the while not knowing whether my son was even alive. I was told that if I left, I'd be considered absent from work, and that that was a fireable offense. Simply asking for paternity leave seemed an act of treason.

I finally resigned myself to the fact that my employer would never approve the paternity leave, so I just left. Thankfully, mother and son recovered. I was able to get a passport too, and two and a half months later, I returned to work. Unbelievably, I was treated like some kind of treasonous villain—a pariah who had betrayed the company. I was stripped of my position and someone else was given my title. Then, I was ignored. Everyone pretended that I wasn't there. It was as if I didn't exist. I wasn't given a new job, or any responsibilities, or even invited to meetings. If I emailed my boss, he didn't respond. If I called him, he didn't pick up the phone.

I tried speaking with HR about the situation, and they kind of patronized me. They told me to go to my boss—my harasser, and the one who took my job away from me in the first place—and commit a kind of *hara wo watte hanasu*, which is the Japanese term for "spill your guts." Basically, HR advised that I humiliate myself in front of my boss, beg his forgiveness, and see what he says. I felt like this must be how they treat women after they come back to work after giving birth. I noted that their treatment of me was illegal, and so they re-invited me to the meetings on a "voluntary" basis. These were, in fact, the same meetings I'd been responsible for convening before taking parental leave. Now they were no longer my meetings, and I wasn't even required to show up. My participation would likely not be welcome at all. I was the outsider, the treasonous one. The unspoken message was, "Real men put the company first, and they don't take paternity leave."

My foreign coworkers and colleagues overseas didn't understand why I was being treated that way, and many of them still don't understand. They were shocked. To this day, I think a lot of them don't really understand what happened and why it happened. The Japanese employees just kind of buried their heads in the sand and went along, believing that if they stood up against leadership's decision, they would be fired. Fear of management was always in the air.

"I believe a culture of discrimination and harassment (particularly against foreigners and women) was condoned by these management members."

"In an atmosphere of fear, harassment and retaliation, everyone was afraid to speak out against Chiharu Abe and Akihiro Kiyomi's leadership. I did, and believe it was a factor in the firm retaliating against me."

"I have never witnessed nor experienced a culture as toxic as the one at MUFG, where threats, harassment, and intimidation were a rampant feature of management."

—SCOTT FUJII, OFFICIAL COURT STATEMENT IN GLEN WOOD'S MORGAN STANLEY AND MITSUBISHI CASE

Mine was, by no means, an isolated case. Another person in the company had a son who developed a growth in his leg. The doctors suspected bone cancer, and they recommended a test to verify the diagnosis. His boss denied him leave—he was told he should sit at his desk and focus on his work tasks, because that was what was expected from "good" employees. Eventually, my friend and his family went back to the doctor to get the test, and his son got better. But after that, the man's boss targeted him, harassing him to the point where he was forced to leave the company. This man was one of the highest value-adding members of his team. What his boss did was an active destruction of value, based on some unspoken rulebook of how employees should behave.

When I look back at that time in my life, I believe that many women had suffered similar treatment from the company before and after it happened to me. I realized that women who dared to start a family and take maternity leave left in one role and came back to work as secretaries. They were never promoted. Their careers were over. I have a very clear recollection of my boss saying to a room full of older Japanese men: "That bitch joined this company just to have babies. Well, we'll teach her a thing or two." And people laughed. I'm not embellishing his words here; this is what he said. I was as shocked to hear it as you are reading it right now. Not just at the language, but at the whole misogynistic concept; at the thought that not only are there men alive today who believe this, but they're bold enough in a group to actually say it. It's appalling. Mitsubishi's vision is to be the "world's most trusted" organization, and this is what its top management is saying behind closed doors.[34] This is what they believe, and they have the power to act on it. Having a child was looked at as a betrayal of the company. I didn't realize that someday I'd be the one they were complaining about, for trying to balance work and family.

Eventually, I was fired. In the meantime, I had suffered through nine months of trying to get them to reinstate my job title and responsibilities to no avail. I became physically exhausted and pushed to the brink mentally by this whole excruciating process. To make matters worse, I now had sole custody of my son and no job. Nor did I have any hopes of being hired by another financial firm in Japan, thanks to what Mitsubishi's top management was saying about me. They had me cornered, and I think they expected me to disappear with my tail between my legs.

---

34 "The MUFG Way," MUFG, accessed January 31, 2023, https://www.mufgemea.com/about-us/values-and-philosophy/.

THE REAL RULEBOOK

Bear in mind, this is not what Mitsubishi Morgan Stanley is telling their investors or the world. On their website home page, in big letters, they say: "At Mitsubishi Morgan Stanley, we strive to create an environment that offers various forms of support for efforts to balance work and private life and have in place a full range of systems that enable both men and women to achieve a balance between work and childrearing."[35] This is their mission statement; this is what they feature in all those glossy brochures (a great example of greenwashing/virtue signaling). And yet, what they do is in stark contrast to this. They fired me for caring about my family, and they pushed out an incredible value-adding employee because he wanted to be with his family during a medical emergency.

This is why we need ESG evaluation standards. It doesn't matter how many CSR brochures you print with smiling families and testimonials about "work-life balance"; every employee knows there's a *real* rulebook. In Mitsubishi Morgan Stanley's unspoken rulebook, asking for paternity leave branded me as treasonous.

But this isn't only about me. It's about the some 200,000 people Mitsubishi employs locally. It's about other global organizations that do the same thing, even if they haven't done it to me. So I asked myself, how do I take this terrible experience and make something good out of it? One way was to start a company based on sustainability, another was to start an sustainable investment fund, and a third was to write this book. Telling this story is painful, but if I tell it, and if I tell other people's stories

---

35 "Towards a Better Working Environment," Mitsubishi Morgan Stanley, accessed January 31, 2023, https://www.sc.mufg.jp/english/company/sustainability/employee_environment.html.

as well, then maybe we can all see that the solution isn't so difficult. And if we embrace the solution, it's going to benefit us all.

My legal case against Mitsubishi Morgan Stanley is still in the courts. They have refused to admit that they did anything wrong, even though everything they did—not telling me about my right to apply for paternity leave, rejecting my application, taking away my job when I returned, demanding a DNA test, destroying evidence while the trial was proceeding, and misleading the court—was and still is illegal. Obviously, firing me was also illegal.

As a side note, there's a sort of "hero story" that's circulated around the company. The hero employee in the tale was on the phone to a client when he suffered a heart attack. The man covered the mouthpiece of the phone and yelled to somebody, "Call an ambulance, I'm having a heart attack." Then he went back to his phone call with the client. The man died at his desk. This isn't a made-up story shared among colleagues for a chuckle. It happened. More disturbing is the fact that employees actually believe this is how they should behave. The company should be their first and only priority; more important than paternity leave, family, and even their own lives.

The case garnered a lot of domestic and global media attention, and I believe it's made a difference in how corporations in Japan treat employees who want time off for family matters, particularly men who request paternity leave. I even got messages from men telling me that when they handed in their applications, they included a copy of an article about my case, and the process went very smoothly, with no questions asked.

Even Mitsubishi instituted a policy that all men *must* take paternity leave.[36] The policy affects about 3,000 men a year at the company. They aren't required to take an extended leave, but they must take some time off.

The CEO of Natural Rights and women's rights activist, Sayaka Osakabe, in a November 3 editorial published on Japan's Yahoo News, took up Wood's court case and lamented that these kinds of incidents were still rampant, noting that demoting parents who returned to the office was a form of harassment. She wrote, "He has great courage (in Japan) to come forward, show his face and talk about this."[37]

The case has cost the company millions of dollars in lawyers' fees. They refuse to admit any wrongdoing and have hired the best lawyers to defend the indefensible. More than the financial cost, the media attention given the case damaged their reputation they claim. The company can't claim to be a family friendly enterprise that cares about society. Prospective employees, customers, and investors think twice about doing business with them. I don't know how the American employees at Morgan Stanley felt about it, but they were most definitely aware of the bad publicity, and that reflected on their business as well. Both companies continue to do damage control. The latest attempt by Morgan Stanley is a video of a woman from

36 "Diversity Management," Mitsubishi Corporation, accessed January 31, 2023, https://mitsubishicorp. disclosure.site/en/themes/120.

37 Sayaka Osakabe, "Why a Senior Manager at Mitsubishi UFJ Morgan Stanley Came Forward to Talk about His Experiences with Paternity Harassment," Yahoo News Japan, November 3, 2017, https://news. yahoo.co.jp/byline/osakabesayaka/20171103-00077698.

their Tokyo office talking about how the company allowed her to have both a career and a family.[38] It's classic damage control, and an attempt to cover up what's going on instead of confronting it and fixing it.

The global securities business that I had built for them was on track to become a $100 million business. After they took away my role and put someone else in charge, that business evaporated. I could have told them that putting someone in charge of a global securities division who didn't speak English well and didn't have my extensive background in global finance was a bad idea, but I don't think they would have listened. Their decision was made out of spite, and because they wanted to set an example for other men who might be thinking of taking paternity leave. (More recently, they have completely thrown in the towel and given the business to Morgan Stanley.)

I do wonder whether there was some jealousy involved. My boss at the time was an older gentleman who had a family, yet he spent very little time at home and had never been allowed to take paternity leave. He may have been bitter seeing me, a foreign employee, come in expecting to attend the birth of my son.

In any case, Mitsubishi Morgan Stanley clearly has a harassment problem. In July 2018, while my court case was in progress, the head of Mitsubishi-UFJ Financial Group, Inc., Saburo Araki, stated as much. In an article in Bloomberg, Araki is quoted as saying, "I have come across several harassment complaints from employees since I arrived...I want to eradicate it, but it will be difficult to root out."[39]

---

38   "Profile: Mia Nagasaka," Morgan Stanley, accessed January 31, 2023, https://www.morganstanley.com/
       profiles/mia-nagasaka-japan-equity-analyst-research.

39   Takahiko Hyuga, "MUFG-Morgan Stanley Venture Chief Vows to Erase Harassment,"
       Bloomberg, July 2, 2018, https://www.bloomberg.com/news/articles/2018-07-02/
       mufg-morgan-stanley-venture-chief-vows-to-stamp-out-harassment.

Indeed, there's a "Mitsubishi Victims Support Group" that has been put together to support victims of harassment from Mitsubishi and Morgan Stanley.

Remember, financial compensation for how I was illegally treated, however deserved, was not the objective. I just wanted Mitsubishi and Morgan Stanley to admit that what they did was wrong; for them to stop destroying other families, and to give me my job back. They still refuse. The company's decision truly makes no sense to me. Not only does it tell the world that Mitsubishi does not care about human rights, which is a poor PR move, but it is also a bad business decision in purely financial terms. Firing me has cost the bank a minimum of $60 million in profit that I could have easily made for them. No matter how you look at it, this was a bad decision, and one which they still have the power to rectify.

Companies must take it upon themselves to prioritize the family, prioritize society, and prioritize their impact. As Nelson Mandela said, "There can be no keener revelation of a society's soul than the way in which it treats its children." As with policies and actions that cause environmental damage, those that cause societal damage lead to decreased profits and other challenges. The old tradition of employees being married to their jobs is no longer viable in our society. People still see their work as a part of their life, but not the focus of their life.

SOCIETY, THE FAMILY, AND BUSINESS OVER TIME

While it's difficult to make gross generalizations about the past, we've gone through periods of time, from culture to culture, where the employer-employee relationship has been damaging to society. In some countries, such as Japan, for a time, the serf-lord relationship worked well and both parties were happy with the arrangement, as long as it was mutually beneficial and there was mutual respect.

A culture that supports both sides and allows freedom and room for the worker to grow mentally, spiritually, physically, and culturally, and allows them to balance their time between work and family can benefit everyone. The worker must be allowed to accomplish career goals and accomplish personal goals outside the company. There are plenty of good companies that have been doing this for a long time.

In the past, companies distanced themselves from social issues. Similar to the division of church and state, they were reluctant to take a stand behind any issue that might be seen as controversial. They were simply businesses in the business of making money, and opinions and interests beyond that did not fit their desired image. Governments, churches, and non-profit enterprises could worry about everything else.

However, the birth of corporate social responsibility (CSR) actually began in the late 1800s when there was growing concern that worker well-being was impacting productivity. Criticism had arisen around the factory system, working conditions, and the employment of women and children, especially in the United States. The consensus was that those employment practices were contributing to poverty, labor unrest, and other social problems.

In 1899, the founder of the US Steel corporation, Andrew Carnegie, wrote *The Gospel of Wealth,* which signaled the emergence of philanthropy. Carnegie donated large portions of his wealth to education and scientific research and established the Carnegie Institute and the Carnegie libraries. John D. Rockefeller, who made most of his money in the oil industry, donated most of his wealth to religious, educational, and scientific causes.

During the 1970s in the United States, the idea of corporate social responsibility was formalized as a sort of social contract between businesses and society. Companies acknowledged that they existed because of public consent, so if the public is consenting to allow companies to function, then companies have an obligation to contribute to society. By the 1980s, CSR began to really take root, and from the 1990s and into the 2000s, there arose a universal acceptance of corporate social responsibility.

Along with the United Nations Sustainable Development Goals (SDGs), CSR has become an essential strategy for organizations. Corporations know that if they don't have a strategy of corporate social responsibility and are not adding value to society, their bottom line will be affected negatively.

The Greek philosopher Heraclitus said, "Character is destiny." A company's culture reflects its character, and I believe that character-driven culture defines its destiny. Companies that treat their employees at least as well as they treat their customers have a brighter future and a sustainable destiny. A company that makes, as its core mission, making fans not only of its customers but also its employees, and that succeeds in that mission, will have an extraordinarily successful and profitable business.

Companies seeking to avoid policies and actions that damage society are moving toward creating CSR divisions. They see the need to incorporate social concerns into their planning and operations. They realize that in addition to maximizing shareholder value, they need to act in a manner that benefits society. This goes beyond philanthropy or donating time and money to popular causes. Giving employees one day off a year to clean up the local park or volunteer at the local soup kitchen isn't enough. Too often, a small percentage of employees participate in those activities—yet they're all wearing company-logoed shirts, and a photo of their efforts ends up in the company brochure. In other words, this kind of effort is nothing more than a photo opportunity of virtue signaling for the company that does little for society.

Some companies that have engaged in nefarious activities in the past have made major strides and come up with the best strategies going forward. Wells Fargo, for example, was exposed during the financial crisis. In that instance, investors took a close look at the bank's business activities and their share price dropped. Wells Fargo made an about face and revamped the company to be in accord with CSR strategies. Other American companies such as Coca-Cola, Walt Disney, and Pfizer came out as corporate social responsibility stalwarts and, in effect, didn't lose the public's trust. The American sports apparel company Nike made headlines by publicly supporting football star Colin Kaepernick and the Black Lives Matter movement.

In Japan, retail giant Marui; baby care company Pigeon, Corp.; beer-brewing company Sapporo Breweries, Ltd; the diaper company, Unicharm; and food company Kewpie have stood out as companies more progressive than most, willing to risk speaking out on corporate social responsibility.

Kewpie, which is famous for their mayonnaise, displays their commitment to CSR on their homepage. The company even lists how they're contributing to the UN's seventeen specific SDGs. For the goal of contributing to a healthy lifespan, for example, they provide menus and recipes. They have open kitchens and encourage employees to bring their children to work to eat with them. Instead of mere lip service, the company has top-down initiatives that are embraced by leadership. Kewpie believes that contributing to a sustainable society is a foundation for their growth as a corporation. When you look at the past activities of many organizations, what Kewpie says is really quite revolutionary.

However, even the most forward-thinking companies show a lack of consistency in their policies. Nike spokesperson Allyson Felix was negotiating maternity protections with the company when she was asked to appear in a female empowerment ad.

The Olympic sprinter called the sports apparel company's request "beyond disrespectful and tone-deaf." Offered a 70 percent pay cut, the pregnant Felix left Nike and joined the women-focused Athleta.[40]

Society cannot be viewed as expendable, or as an unlimited resource. It is not acceptable to use and abuse it as long as you're making money. Again, the power of circles shows us that every decision has an impact, and that impact is not finite. Like a circle, the ramifications of poor decisions that damage society are widespread, like ripples, and those ripples impact the company and its leadership.

Figure 5.3

40 Sean Gregory, "Motherhood Could Have Cost Olympian Allyson Felix. She Wouldn't Let It," *Time*, July 8, 2021, https://time.com/6077124/allyson-felix-tokyo-olympics/.

Businesses that see the value in society and that operate in ways that benefit society will be more sustainable. Those that go after their goals in a linear fashion with no consideration for their societal impact will either be forced to evolve into more sustainable organizations, or they will eventually cease to exist (in other words, embrace defeat).[41]

If we give companies the benefit of the doubt and assume that their bad actions aren't intentional, but that leadership is simply unaware of their impact on society, then rather than chastise them, we can look at ideas like ESG, SDGs, and CSR as a corrective mechanism for businesses gone awry in the pursuit of profit. So, they got the money-making part of capitalism right; they just lost their way when it came to contributing to society.

RISKS AND BENEFITS ASSOCIATED WITH BECOMING A SOCIETY- AND FAMILY-FRIENDLY COMPANY

The United Nations Sustainable Development Goals, or SDGs, listed in the introduction of this book, include goals that directly impact society and the family, which can be promoted through company policy and action. Recall, from that list, goal 7, "good health and well-being"; goal 9, "gender equality"; goal 12, "decent work and economic growth"; and goal 14, "reduced inequalities." These goals that benefit society and the family aren't in any way a sacrifice that business must make to society. Indeed, they are the way forward for operating and managing a sustainable corporation. Companies that fail to incorporate

---

41   Embrace defeat is a reference to *Embracing Defeat*, a fantastic history book by John W. Dower about Japanese culture and accepting defeat after war.

these goals into their business strategy will find it difficult to survive, while those that embrace them will find sustainable success.

I believe this movement is only going to accelerate. I don't think we're going backwards. If a company continues to operate at the expense of society, their cost of doing business is going to skyrocket. They won't be able to get the capital they need to continue. On the financial side, it will become difficult for them to survive. The damage to their reputation will make it impossible for them to compete.

Companies that benefit society, on the other hand, have everything to gain. They will still have to create and provide a value-added product or service, and they will still have to be profitable, but they will have to do so with a strong focus on corporate social responsibility (CSR). They will have to treat society as a renewable resource that needs to be nurtured, developed, and restored. Companies that do this will have lower financial costs of capital, at least in part thanks to ESG investing. Investors—whether they are large, long-term institutional investors, or pensioners—want to invest in sustainable companies. If a company has sustainable policies in place, then this will dramatically increase their flow of capital and decrease their costs of doing business. But if they have a reputation for unsustainability and scandals, then their costs of doing business are only going to rise. Investors that do true due diligence on their investments have always known this and have done the required research into the companies they choose to own.

Sustainable companies are the organizations of the future. Per the very definition of the word "sustainable," that should go without saying. They will have better relationships with their customers. They will attract better quality employees. They will create a positive, upward spiral, increasing their competitiveness, sustainability, and profitability. They are the companies that will last.

KEY TAKEAWAY

Companies, and especially large corporations, are now embracing corporate social responsibility. They have realized that it's not enough to put out expensive virtue signaling brochures illustrating all the "wonderful" things they're supposedly doing for society, nor to produce flashy corporate websites that overpromise and underdeliver. Empty platitudes are by definition meaningless. That green-washing era has come to an end, and corporations now have to put their money where their mouth is. They need to have a corporate social responsibility strategy, and incorporate it into their business in concrete ways that are demonstrable, where shareholders can actually see the difference the company is making. Shareholders are asking specific ESG questions, and companies must now compete for a broad range of resources, including financial and human capital, based on these ESG criteria. It's a very new world.

A friend of mine was the head of a California-based foundation comprising a community of Japanese and US business leaders. One of the foundation's sponsors was a large Japanese banking corporation. My friend makes regular visits to the sponsors. On a visit with the top management of this bank, she asked them about their CSR strategy. Out came a beautiful brochure, and the managers began pointing at the images and explaining each one. After twenty minutes of explaining the photographs and articles in the brochure, my friend looked each manager in the eye and said, "So, tell me specifically what you've done over the past year for CSR." The room went silent, and she was angry. She still is...

"You know this isn't CSR," she said. "It's a fancy brochure. It's marketing." She made very clear to them what she thought of their brochure. Her foundation severed the relationship with that sponsor.

The era of pretending to care is over. The time for brochures has come to an end. If you're not doing something that's real and tangible and demonstrable, claims that you care about society are meaningless. You can no longer fool shareholders. The public is very serious about this. Governments are serious about it and the United Nations is serious about it. Corporate responsibility to society isn't a passing fad that will go out of style. It began in the late 1800s, and though it took a while to gain serious traction, we are now at a point where businesses that don't take it seriously are going to be in trouble.

GUIDED REFLECTIONS:

1. What is the CSR policy at your business?

   ....

2. How is CSR incorporated as a pillar of your growth strategy for the foreseeable future?

   ....

3. Looking at society as a valuable resource, how much are you using and what are you giving back?

   ....

4. If you were audited for CSR and had to show how you spent the last year's budget, would you produce a brochure, or would you have a real story about the difference your business is making to society?

   ....

5. Do you have a third-party audit process for your social/ management practices?

....

6. What is your parental leave policy? Are you following up with the line management to assure it is being followed?

....

7. Do you have a whistleblower protection policy? Is it working? Proof?

....

8. What is your corporate harassment policy? How is it working? Is it audited by third parties?

....

9. Do you have a separate, unspoken rulebook in your company? Why, or why not? If yes, how does the unspoken rulebook differ from your written rulebook?

....

10. How does your unspoken rulebook serve your organization? How, indeed, does it serve your customers?

....

11. Is your unspoken rulebook in line with your business strategy, or is it just the remains of the past that might be dragging your company down?

....

12. If your "unspoken" rule book were to appear on the front page of the Wall Street Journal, would it help or hinder your brand?

....

CHAPTER 6

CORPORATE GOVERNANCE

"Corporate governance is concerned with holding the balance between economic and social goals and between individual and communal goals. The governance framework is there to encourage the efficient use of resources and equally to require accountability for the stewardship of those resources."

—SIR ADRIAN CADBURY

The Enron accounting scandal led to one of the largest bankruptcies in US history. It also led to huge changes in accounting standards and practices. The scandal also embroiled one of the largest auditing firms in the world, Arthur Andersen. When the story broke, the news dominated the financial world and was covered by global media.

Enron held more than $60 billion in assets at the time. Under increasing competition, the company had cut corners in an effort to catch up to their competitors. They did this by using mark-to-market accounting to basically "cook the books" and make things look better than they were. This drove up the share price because investors weren't getting the true picture of the company's actual financial standing.

Before the scandal, Enron saw their profits shrinking as competition was heating up. The share price started to waver, and shareholders were getting upset with the company. They wanted to know what was going on with their investments. Under that pressure, instead of looking for legal ways to improve the business, they began using mark-to-market accounting to hide the troubles and paint a picture that was much different than the actual status. Mark-to-market accounting allowed them to write unrealized future gains from some trading contracts into the current income statements, giving the illusion of higher current profits.

On top of that, Enron pulled their troubled divisions that weren't performing well out of the company and put them into Special Purpose Entities or Vehicles, which are referred to as SPEs or SPVs (pronounced *spivs*, which is funny considering they are essentially spivvy). SPEs or SPVs are limited partnerships created with outside parties. By doing this, Enron was able to remove all their underperforming business and troubled assets from the company's balance sheet. They were still responsible for that business and those assets, but they were "off the books" so to speak, making their losses appear fewer and their income, better.

The CFO at the time was Andrew Fastow and the CEO and founder of Enron was Ken Lay. Due to the scandal, Lay's name became a household name. Fastow managed some of the SPEs himself. If they had been managed by a third party, Arthur Andersen may have not been aware of them, but because they were still under the management of Enron's CFO, Arthur Andersen should have been aware that they were still owned by Enron and had simply been sold off. The corruption at Enron was top-down driven from the executive level and through the ranks. Everyone down the line took their marching orders and did as they were told.

In many ways, this is similar to what I faced at Mitsubishi Morgan Stanley. Everyone knew that what was happening to me was wrong, but they also knew that if they spoke up, their lives would be destroyed. It made it difficult for people to do the right thing. Sitting down, shutting up, and following marching orders was—and still is—the easiest way to survive. It's company policy, and it's the "real" rule book.

When no one speaks up in an organization, it's a clear sign of corporate governance and leadership problems. Remember, our definition of leaders are people who fight to do the right thing. If company policy requires people to fall in line, then the concept of leadership cannot thrive. You're essentially hiring a bunch of managers to do what they're told. Companies spend so much money recruiting, onboarding, and hiring the best talent they can—why bother if these people aren't empowered to fulfill their potential?

Sustainable organizations have policies in place to give their employees a voice. And I don't mean the standard toll-free number for anonymous complaints. This may have been a great idea fifty years ago, but it's proved unsustainable. Many companies just record the complaints, forward them to the accused and/or to top management, and the person who spoke up is reprimanded or fired. In other words, it's a trap. Companies need whistleblower protection programs. They must show they're serious about listening and making change. If not, you'll end up with an organization that's full of managers capable of keeping quiet and following orders but not much else—the definition of rats on a sinking ship and the antithesis of what we would call sustainable.

Before the scandal, Enron stock was around $90 a share. By November 2001, it had dropped to $1. The crime didn't only affect shareholders, who lost a lot of money, it also destroyed Enron employees' pension plans, which were tied to the stock price. Their 401(k) plans became worthless. Destruction of value is the price of "shutting up," and the price increases dramatically if left to fester. In the case of Enron, it led to jail time.

The SEC investigated, Fastow was fired, and others resigned. Federal lawsuits followed, along with hundreds of civil suits. Shareholders wanted both Enron and Arthur Andersen to be held accountable for misleading them into putting their money into a company based on false financials.

Wall Street analysts were among the first to notice something was wrong at Enron. The publicly released financial statements didn't make sense to them. Prompted by a whistleblower within Enron, an internal investigation followed. SEC investigators were particularly interested in the transactions that had occurred between Enron and the SPEs managed by CFO Fastow. Arguably, the SEC should have questioned that arrangement much sooner—so why didn't they? It's hard to believe that this went unchecked for so long without someone on the inside knowing and letting it go on.

Fastow was initially charged with ninety-eight counts of fraud, money laundering, insider trading, conspiracy, and other crimes. He pled guilty to two charges of conspiracy and was sentenced to ten years in prison with no parole. CEO Lay was indicted on six felony counts, which prosecutors later dismissed in favor of a single misdemeanor tax charge.

Both men's wives were also charged. Sixteen people in all pled guilty for crimes committed at Enron, and five others, including four former Merrill Lynch employees, were found guilty. Eight former Enron executives testified, including the main witness, Fastow. In the end, many lives were changed, some destroyed. Enron went bankrupt and Arthur Andersen was dissolved.

CORPORATE GOVERNANCE: THE G IN ESG

Recall that the "g" in ESG—Environmental, Social, and Governance goals—refers to corporate governance. Every country has corporate structure rules, laws, and reporting requirements central to the formation and governance of a corporation. Corporations hire and manage people. Their actions impact employees, customers, and investors. A corporation's adherence to those governance rules dictates that impact to a degree, and sometimes, as in the case of Enron, a lack of adherence can be devastating.

Corporate governance also affects revenue reporting and corporate taxes, which impacts society. When a business doesn't pay its fair share, taxes that could be collected and used to develop a country's infrastructure, schools, and other government resources are short-changed. But those resources still need to be developed, and so governments often fund them through tax hikes on individuals. In other words, it's us who pay the price. The economy suffers as well because individuals drive consumption, and now, they have less money in their pockets to spend thanks to these higher taxes. Would a flat-tax policy perhaps eliminate the corporate tax loopholes and billionaire tax dodges, forcing all businesses and individuals to pay their fair share? Might it also put more money in the hands of consumers, positively impacting consumption, the major driver of the economy?

Corporate structure impacts society. Since corporations are allowed to exist because of public consent, those institutions should therefore be transparent in how they're managed. All stakeholders have a right to know how those companies are organized and how decisions are made. The public also has a right to know what the company's finances truly look like; how people are hired, treated, and fired; how employees are promoted into executive levels; and how new employees are hired into those positions.

Stakeholders have a right to information about a public corporation's board of directors and outside directors too, including who they are, what they do, and how much they're paid. Without this kind of transparency, a person at a high level could hire a friend, colleague, or family member to a high-paying job, even if the person had no credentials and is unable to add value to the business.

The Enron disaster led to new regulations and legislation around financial reporting for public companies. The Sarbanes–Oxley Act of 2002 increased the penalties for fabricating financial records. The corporate community should be embarrassed that we even need a law like that, but Enron proved its necessity. Investors were duped out of a lot of money. People's lives were devastated, their retirements obliterated. So many today are still suffering from the fallout of the Enron catastrophe.

Our opinion is that corporate governance is the most important part of ESG. In fact, I prefer the term GSE to ESG, because corporate governance is an order of magnitude more important than social and environmental policies.

What do we mean by transparent corporate governance? Today, companies are claiming ESG strategies and a commitment to SDGs, but with no real data to back up their claims. In other words, they have no evidence of any concrete action. There's even a name for the phenomenon: "green-washing." Junta Nakai, Global Industry Leader for Financial Services at Databricks, offers a great example:

> A recent 70-page sustainability report from a leading investment bank had just three pages dedicated to hard metrics. The remaining 67 pages undoubtedly contain valuable information and signals. But how does an investor or client of this bank quantify the text to objectively quantify ESG performance? Do these disclosures reflect the reality of ESG performance or are they simply the easiest observable data points?

> This phenomenon is well documented in what is called "greenwashing," a term designated to institutions that mislead consumers/investors about the performance of their ESG goals.[42]

In other words, sixty-seven pages of that report were fluff and three pages were dedicated to useful information. That needs to change. Fancy brochures are not going to cut it in this day and age. If companies are serious about corporate governance, then they must implement measures that prove their commitment, and be transparent about it not only to their shareholders, but also to their employees, partners, and customers. Otherwise, "when there is little distinction between stated

---

42 Junta Nakai, "The Best Way for Companies to Incorporate ESG Goals Is by Using Data Science and AI," Business Insider India, July 10, 2020, https://www.businessinsider.in/finance/news/the-best-way-for-companies-to-incorporate-esg-goals-is-by-using-data-science-and-ai/articleshow/76900315.cms.

ESG goals and supporting facts, the ESG movement risks losing its meaning and impact."[43]

This is, in fact, already the case. In the US market, for example, many companies claim to have an ESG strategy, or be ESG-compliant, or even to be leading the way on ESG in America. They can get away with these statements due to the lack of defined ESG standards. There is no tool for measuring a company's ESG standing, progress, or degree of compliance. Sure, there's a Bloomberg ESG score, a Yahoo ESG score, and an MSCI ESG score. Each one has their own unique way of measuring ESG, their own standards by which to deem a company compliant. Without real data from the company that's organized, clear, and judged by a universal standard, a company's claim of ESG compliance is, at best, questionable.

So how do we demand transparency and how do companies properly implement it? Nakai suggests three salient points: (1) more frequent reporting, (2) checking companies' ESG disclosures, and (3) making sure those companies are held accountable. All three of these points will play a big role in holding companies up to ESG standards and avoiding green-washing. As Nakai says, "Leaders don't just talk about sustainability. They act on it."[44]

Companies themselves must commit to this transparency and provide hard data to back up their claims. Businesses like Marui are leading the revolution with data books, reports that are neither colorful nor fancy but simply collections of hard data. Marui's book is not three pages; it is twenty-five pages on their policies and results in minute detail that can be ana-

43   Nakai, "Best Way for Companies to Incorporate ESG."

44   Junta Nakai, "Suite to Site: Why Companies Fail to Achieve Climate Goals," *Chief Data Officer Magazine*, May 26, 2021, https://www.cdomagazine.tech/cdo_magazine/news_feed/stories/suite-to-site-why-companies-fail-to-achieve-climate-goals/article_bded7eee-bee5-11eb-bc76-e7e309ad71bb.html.

lyzed, traced back, and verified. This is what we mean when we talk about real transparency and real action taken towards ESG strategies and SDGs. "In the end, data brings transparency. Transparency empowers action. Action generates data. This is the flywheel that could quite literally save the world."[45]

The onus is on senior management and those at the executive level to maintain this transparency. After all, they are paid much more than the average employee. The public expects people at those levels to take responsibility to ensure the company is run in an ethical, honest way that they are proud of and not ashamed to share. Because of the recent popularity of ESG, corporate governance has gained attention. Corporate leaders must be prepared to answer tough questions. They must be vigilant in how they manage a business and how they clearly and consistently communicate with shareholders.

Part of having a healthy and transparent system of corporate governance is a good whistleblower protection program. You'll be surprised by the number of companies for whom saving face is far more important than correcting past wrongs. In 2011, for example, Japan saw a huge scandal when Michael Woodford, the newly appointed foreign CEO of Olympus, blew the whistle on fraud and corruption in the company. "Oddly," William Pesek writes, "the company's board seemed more upset over Woodford going public than the malfeasance itself. He was shown the door and claimed to face death threats."[46]

In other words, Olympus would rather have had the $1.7 billion malfeasance continue than reveal it to the public. This is why good whistleblower protection programs are essential—

45 Nakai, "Suite to Site."

46 William Pesek, "Tokyo Circles the Wagons around Toshiba," opinion, *Nikkei Asia*, June 21, 2021, https://asia.nikkei.com/Opinion/Tokyo-circles-the-wagons-around-Toshiba.

they ensure your employees are empowered to speak up, that companies are not scheming to cook the books or commit fraud instead of adding value to society, and that shareholders are adequately protected.

Much has changed around corporate governance since the collapse of Enron. Today, compliance with regulations around business and financial expectations is a matter of course. The bottom line is that in order to ensure sustainability and long-term viability of any business, and especially a public corporation, transparency in governance is key.

CORPORATE GOVERNANCE OVER TIME

Corporate governance encompasses board structure, managerial accountability, and shareholder rights. The history of corporate governance goes all the way back to the sixteenth and seventeenth centuries with the first large trading companies, such as the East India Company and the Hudson's Bay Company. While the concept of corporate governance has existed for centuries, the idea of ethical corporate governance didn't emerge until the 1970s.

In the United States, corporate governance began as a discussion around the balance of power, and more specifically, decision-making among corporate boards of directors, executive and management teams, and shareholders. Later, customers also became part of the discussion as a fourth group in this balance of power. The question as to who has the most decision-making power—and who should have the most power—has been a hot topic for decades among academics, regulators, executives, and investors. Determining the right balance, and regulating that balance, has become quite complicated, and the rules vary from country to country.

Official SEC corporate governance reforms in the 1970s eventually led to the Protection of Shareholders Rights Act in 1980. The 1980s is often referred to as the Deal Decade, with a lot of takeovers and other large deals between businesses that led to shareholder issues. Investors wanted to know the value of the companies they'd invested in that had been bought, sold, and merged. These questions drove further reform and regulations.

Economic growth during the 1990s proved to be fertile ground for scandals, and the recessions that followed tended to expose them. It seemed that as long as share prices went up and everyone was making money, no one was questioning how it was being made. When share prices went down, shareholders wanted to know why. The Enron scandal came to light soon after the high-tech bubble burst and 9/11. Likewise, market maker Bernie Madoff's massive Ponzi scheme that bilked investors out of billions of dollars went unchecked until shortly after the Great Financial Crisis began in late 2007. Through economic expansion and contraction, when the tide goes out, you discover who is and who is not "wearing pants."

These financial crises of the early part of the twenty-first century led to more federal regulations in the US, including the Sarbanes–Oxley Act of 2002, and the Dodd–Frank Wall Street Reform and Consumer Protection Act of 2010. Aside from formal laws, people who sat on the boards of large corporations felt the pressure to take more responsibility for how companies operated, and actually do something about the problems instead of merely participating in a monthly call and collecting a huge salary.

CORPORATE GOVERNANCE IN THE TWENTY-FIRST CENTURY

Though corporate governance codes and standards vary from country to country, we are slowly moving toward global standardization. Today, strong corporate governance demands that corporations have a percentage of independent and diverse directors. Diversity and independence of corporate governance and the board of directors means more than representation across genders, races, ages, and educational backgrounds. Members should be truly independent of one another, unlike past decades where a CEO could put his or her girlfriend or boyfriend in that role. Since 2008, those roles have come under greater scrutiny. The overall composition of the board, as well, is more closely scrutinized.

Diversity across the aforementioned demographics, as well as industry diversity, is encouraged. For example, a technology company should seek to have not only representatives from the tech industry on its board, but people with financial, accounting, and entrepreneurial expertise should also be considered for these roles. Independence and diversity influence how the company is governed and how decisions are made, from products and services offered, to growth, profitability, and the impact of these decisions on shareholders. There is also, in turn, an impact on environmental and social concerns. If companies get corporate governance right, ESG problems dissipate, and goals are more easily met.

Among common governance issues are matter of conflicts of interest. If a CEO is incentivized solely on quarterly or annual profits, how likely are they to pay attention to environmental and social issues that may benefit company performance and viability over the longer term? The CEO may be inclined to make decisions that negatively impact ESG goals so that they receive their maximum bonus, and by the time their bad decisions impact the company, they've moved on to another company or retired, leaving a trail of destruction. What looks like short-term gains may in fact be destroying the company, and that destruction may only become apparent after the CEO gets rich and moves on.

This leads to the blame game. After a recent Toshiba scandal, the current CEO went on record to claim he had nothing to do with the whole affair—it was the fault of the last CEO. Does this sound like a true leader to you? Leaders take responsibility for what happens in their organization—always. They step up. Taking responsibility is not only an attribute of a leader, but also an action that leads to sustainability. What you have today, however, is top management acting like managers, not leaders. Their primary goal is to shirk responsibility and they're always looking for someone to blame. Indeed, "leaders" in large Japanese corporations like Toshiba and Mitsubishi are taught to never, ever find themselves in a position where they have to take responsibility. If they do, they've done something very wrong.

All this comes down to inadequate corporate governance and dysfunctional company culture. People who do take responsibility in these organizations are punished. They're penalized for acting like leaders and not silently following orders, so now you have a whole generation of top management focused on finding scapegoats. This blame game is not sustainable; it leads to scandals and poor decisions. It destroys value.

There is plenty of responsibility to go around. Whoever sets executive compensation goals is responsible. Executives are responsible. Employees, too, who decide to work for companies with poor governance records, as well as investors who put their money in such companies and customers who patronize them.

Auditors, as we have seen in the case of Arthur Andersen, are also accountable for corporate governance.

There needs to be a deeper understanding of the impact of governance throughout the corporation, as well as through the ecosystem of the company and consumers. If a consumer knows that buying a certain product contributes to the destruction of the environment, or that it hurts society in some way, then they too are responsible for that negative impact. If they enjoy these products despite knowing the impact, they are, in a sense, complicit.

Corporate governance education is needed throughout the public enterprise system. Leaders and management should know which practices to follow in their countries and industries and how they, as employees, are accountable. That includes protection for whistleblowers, who should never be punished and must be sheltered. A telltale sign of a company with governance problems is employees who are afraid to speak up. We've seen great examples of this already in Mitsubishi Morgan Stanley and Enron.

Corporate governance should be led by senior management and socialized by either HR, an SDG- or ESG-focused division, or a CSR division. Employee education at all levels is just as critical to ensure people understand their individual responsibilities and their rights. In multinational corporations, it's especially critical to ensure that people understand the different regulations for each country in which they operate. An email that's acceptable in one country may cross regulatory guidelines in another. An employee needs to know those guidelines before they click "send."

Regulations regarding information, including corporate governance-related information and client information that can be sent across borders, varies between countries. In some countries, sharing client information across divisions isn't legal. An employee may first need written permission from the client. This is why education is so important. An uninformed employee in marketing, for example, might not think twice about discussing a client with an employee in research and development or with a marketing colleague at a site in another country. Yet, they could be breaking regulations.

Looking back at the Enron scandal and how much that cost employees in pensions and employment, should serve as motivation for anyone to take it upon themselves to request information about these matters from their leadership. They should never be afraid to speak up when that information is withheld.

Governing a business linearly, focused simply on achieving a goal, won't satisfy the requirements of transparent corporate governance. Leadership must acknowledge the impact of their decisions and work toward a sustainable model through diligent communication and education.

Corporations don't have to go bankrupt or face dissolution. They can survive for many generations, make sizable profits, and contribute to society. Focusing on short-term share prices and the compensation of a few select employees—because yes, even the CEO is an employee—is a recipe for an ESG disaster. Linear thinking and linear versions of corporate governance will undoubtedly conflict with the long-term goals of building a sustainable business that benefits shareholders, employees, and customers, while meeting the goals of corporate governance, society, and the environment. Corporations need to remember: Diversity is a reality, but inclusion is a choice. Management is a reality, but harassment is a choice. Families are a reality, but prioritizing families is a choice. They need to make the right choices and build companies that allow their employees and customers to do the same.

RISKS AND BENEFITS ASSOCIATED WITH ETHICAL AND TRANSPARENT CORPORATE GOVERNANCE

By now, the potential for disaster for those who neglect to abide by governance best practices are obvious. Bankruptcy, dissolution, fines, and jail time are serious deterrents. To a lesser degree, a company risks losing value, losing investors, and losing people. They risk damage to their reputation too. The cost of equity goes up, and the ability to remain competitive decreases.

Toshiba was recently caught in a huge corporate governance scandal, which involved the "145-year-old conglomerate collud[ing] with government officials to block activist investors."[47] Effissimo Capital Management, a Singapore-based hedge fund and one of Toshiba's largest shareholders, was pushing the company to make changes to its board of directors. Although Toshiba is technically duty-bound to listen to its shareholders, management was reluctant to implement these changes. So it did the worst thing possible, not only by good corporate governance standards but also by ethical standards—it conspired with the Japanese Ministry of Economy, Trade and Industry (METI) to bully its shareholders into backing down.

The conspiracy was unearthed by an independent investigation, which found that "Toshiba had 'devised a plan to effectively prevent shareholders from exercising their shareholder proposal right and voting rights,' by putting undue influence on Effissimo, the Harvard fund and another fund, 3D Investment Partners."[48] In the words of a Toshiba executive: "We will ask METI to beat them up for a while."[49]

---

47   Pesek, "Tokyo Circles the Wagons around Toshiba."

48   Makiko Yamazaki, "'Beat Them Up': Toshiba and Japan Colluded Against Foreign Investors, Probe Finds," Reuters, June 10, 2021, https://www.reuters.com/world/asia-pacific/independent-probe-says-toshiba-agm-last-year-was-not-fairly-managed-2021-06-10/.

49   Yamazaki, "'Beat Them Up.'"

This is appalling behavior. It's certainly bad corporate governance and it is definitely anti-capitalistic. It's not even communist behavior, to be honest—it's highway robbery. If the government wants to have a say in how Toshiba runs, then it needs to own Toshiba. Here, it was basically stealing from other people by taking away those rights that the shareholders have paid for. The Japanese government's reaction to the scandal is also very telling. Industry minister Hiroshi Kajiyama pretended nothing was wrong, that a mountain was being made out of a molehill. "Not a problem," he said. "No need to investigate Toshiba scandal."[50] In other words, the government brushed it under the carpet. According to them, this was the normal way of doing business. The "nothing to see here" strategy is unabashedly applied once again.

And perhaps, once upon a time, it was. Like the *yakuza*, Japanese society has what is called *sokaiya*, which is a mafia associated with corporations. *Sokaiya* in Japanese means "general meeting fixer" and these gangs were responsible for controlling shareholders:

> The emergence of these extortionists [the *sokaiya*] was possible because of the wide and permanent gap between the formal reality and the substantial reality in the business world. Since Japanese firms officially have shareholders, shareholder meetings are necessary so as not to disturb this formal reality. In actual reality, the joint stock companies have never had any intention of giving shareholders outside the directorates of their own corporate groups a voice of any kind whatsoever. The *sokaiya's* purpose was to ensure this situation could be maintained.[51]

50 Pesek, "Tokyo Circles the Wagons around Toshiba."

51 Karel van Wolferen, *The Enigma of Japanese Power: People and Politics in a Stateless Nation* (New York: Alfred A. Knopf, 1990), 105.

In other words, Japan's traditional way of doing business is anti-capitalistic and antidemocratic. It is to *pretend* a democratic way of functioning, but, in reality, act in an autocratic manner. An article in the German newspaper *Süddeutsche Zeitung* called this "state-controlled capitalism." They write:

> Independent observers see recent events at Toshiba as a sign of progress. Japan's stiff, state-controlled capitalism is facing headwinds. "Five years ago it would have been impossible for such an objective report to come to the public in such detail," says Nicholas Benes, head of the non-profit organization Board Director Training Institute of Japan. Only the Japanese government does not seem to want to learn any lessons from the thunderstorm.[52]

To me, "state-controlled" and "capitalism" don't go together; it's an oxymoron. The whole point of capitalism is free enterprise. So how can "state-controlled capitalism" still be capitalism? And if this is what Japan or other nations are known for, then they're on the path to unsustainability and, ultimately, failure. This oxymoron is going to make ultra-morons out of the Japanese government and its economy; it's going to lead them towards embracing defeat, as the title of this book says.

---

52 Thomas Hahn, "Welcher Skandal?," *Süddeutsche Zeitung*, June 16, 2021, https://www-sueddeutsche-de.cdn.ampproject.org/c/s/www.sueddeutsche.de/wirtschaft/toshiba-skandal-1.5324345!amp.

EMBRACING DEFEAT

As noted earlier, "embracing defeat" is a reference to John W. Dower's *Embracing Defeat*, a book about post-war Japan. After World War II, the country struggled—and continues to struggle—with its culture and identity. They lost the war to a capitalistic, democratic power, and their constitution was essentially rewritten for them by foreigners. It makes sense that they now have a state-controlled capitalistic system comprising a mishmash of pre- and post-war systems. Today, Japan continues to struggle with democracy and capitalism.

The scandal at Toshiba is a prime example of this. A government interfering in a private company's voting process, meddling with their shareholders, exerting pressure to get the outcome they think is "best" for Japan—that's deeply unsustainable behavior (not to mention illegal and immoral). Maybe in the past, the Japanese government has been able to hide its interference and so had gotten away with it. But they can't hide it anymore. Not in this day and age. It's going to be in the newspapers and on the internet, and it will have severe consequences.

Because of this, Toshiba's reputation has suffered a major blow. People will be hesitant about buying Toshiba shares, and investors will run for the door. You invest in a company for part ownership, and so you can have a say. You put money into a corporation with the understanding that the leadership that's been hired through careful evaluation is going to act in the best interest of the shareholders. If the Japanese government is just going to swoop in and steal that say from you, why bother investing in the business? And if the Japanese government is doing this across Japanese corporations, why bother investing in Japan at all?

For workers who choose to stay with a troubled businesses like Toshiba and Enron, morale tanks and with it, productivity. The best talent does not want to work with a poorly governed business, and even average employees will be looking for employment elsewhere.

This is the domino effect of bad corporate governance. Toshiba and the Japanese government both talk about SDGs and ESG strategies, but if this is how they are behaving, then they don't understand the concept of sustainability at all. Their behavior is unacceptable in today's world. They don't get to wear the SDG lapel pins until they take action and make real progress.

The benefits to ethical and transparent corporate governance are just as obvious. For one, you're more likely to stay in business and not wind up in prison. The cost of equity is lower, as is the cost of attracting and maintaining quality talent. Your brand doesn't suffer, so your marketing costs are less too. With a coordinated approach to communicating the importance of governance to your company and to all stakeholders, from investors to staff to customers, you have a common language that everyone understands and respects.

Imagine how a leader's staff, family, and peers view a company with those kinds of values. Imagine how people at an ethically sound corporation feel about coming to work, and how they view their leadership. Imagine what it feels like to attend a conference where everyone knows that you represent the highest ideals of a public corporation.

Those feelings permeate a company that prioritizes corporate governance. People are proud to work for a company like that, and it shows in productivity, innovation, and retention rates. These are all good things for morale and for profitability.

Finally, sound corporate governance fosters trust. Customers are more likely to trust your company and your people. Your people are more likely to trust management, and management will trust senior leadership. Investment firms will have confidence in your business and will see you as a lower risk investment that isn't going to surprise them with a scandal that tanks your stock price. Transparent and forthright corporate governance creates a circle of trust among all the stakeholders in the corporation. From this circle of trust ripples circles of productivity, sustainability, cooperation, and efficiency.

KEY TAKEAWAY

Corporate governance varies widely between corporations and even within them. The education process may be well conceived and executed at one company, and hodgepodge at another. There is no consistent process for the education of public companies and their employees. However, leadership that understands the risks, the benefits, and even the basics is in a position to prioritize the matter within their company and commit to including it in their charter.

Failing to prioritize corporate governance leads to a whole host of problems, as we've seen with Enron and Toshiba. Companies and governments that continue to dismiss good corporate governance will face fraud, scandals, and immeasurable loss to their reputations. As William Pesek puts it in his article on the Toshiba scandal: "Now, the only thing Toshiba can claim to be the best at is reminding the globe that Japan, Inc. still answers to nobody. And, in some ways, remains as lost as ever."[53]

---

53   William Pesek, "Tokyo Circles the Wagons around Toshiba," opinion, *Nikkei Asia*, June 21, 2021, https://asia.nikkei.com/Opinion/Tokyo-circles-the-wagons-around-Toshiba.

I understand what Pesek is trying to say, but I also think there is hope for companies like Toshiba and for Japan. I see positive change in the cards, and I believe there will be a lot more of it in the future. But for that to happen, companies like Toshiba and governments around the world must embrace what we're discussing in this book. And we don't mean just wearing an SDG lapel pin and pretending to care, but genuinely incorporating sustainable business practices, starting with honest and transparent corporate governance.

If you're an employee or a leader at Toshiba, at Johnson and Johnson, at Mitsubishi, at Morgan Stanley, at Toyota, or at any company looking to survive long into the future, then we challenge you to prove William Pesek wrong. Don't just give up and become a lost corporation, as Pesek predicts. Embrace sustainability and what it has to offer. Make the change within your business and watch as the true value you add to the world generates outsized profits.

GUIDED REFLECTIONS:

1. Can you look your leadership in the eye and have an honest discussion about corporate governance? What about all the people who work for you?

....

2. Are there any red flags in your company around corporate governance? What will you do to correct them?

....

3. How is corporate governance communicated within your company? Who owns the process?

....

4. Does your staff understand their responsibility in corporate governance?

....

5. How are you promoting corporate governance to your customers?

    ....

6. Where does the corporate governance buck stop at your organization?

    ....

7. Are you seeing the benefits of good corporate governance? Why or why not?

    ....

8. Is there an open discussion within the company regarding what corporate governance is and how it affects everyone?

    ....

CHAPTER 7

INVESTORS

"Behind every stock is a company. Find out what it's doing."

—PETER LYNCH

"Goodness is the only investment that never fails."

—HENRY DAVID THOREAU

Japanese automaker Nissan translates to "made in Japan" or "born in Japan" in Japanese. The kanji (character) 日 or *ni*, means "sun" as in *Nihon*, Japan, the "land of the rising sun." The second kanji in Nissan, 産,means "production." The company name indicates that Nissan is the flagship automobile of Japan.

For many years, Nissan leadership held to extraordinarily traditional Japanese management practices. People in high positions were more concerned with protecting themselves and their friends instead of running the business as a business should be run. As a result, Nissan nearly went bankrupt. Uncertain as to the next step, the company's leadership looked to management in other countries to help save the failing automaker.

Figure 7.1

Nissan's leaders brought in Brazilian businessman Carlos Ghosn, formerly with Renault, the French automaker. Ghosn introduced what he called the Nissan Revival Plan, which aimed for a profit margin of 4 to 5 percent by the year 2000, and a 50 percent drop in debt by 2002. To get there, Ghosn cut 14 percent of Nissan's total workforce—that's 21,000 jobs, mostly in Japan—shut down five Japanese plants, and auctioned off several of the company's beloved assets, such as its Aerospace Unit. He also restructured Nissan, cutting the number of suppliers, abolishing seniority-based promotions, and dismantling the corrupt Keiretsu system of cross shareholding. People called him the "Keiretsu Killer" (or "Le Cost Killer" in honor of his first language being French).[54]

His plan worked. Nissan's net profits climbed to $2.7 billion in the first year of the Nissan Revival Plan—a huge jump from the *loss* of $6.46 billion in the previous year. And in only three years, Nissan's operating margins were nearly double the indus-

---

54 *Merriam-Wester* defines "keiretsu" as "a powerful alliance of Japanese businesses often linked by cross-shareholding," https://www.merriam-webster.com/dictionary/keiretsu.

try average, at 9 percent. Ghosn was seen as a miracle worker, heralded not only for saving the automaker but for being a sort of savior of Corporate Japan as well. They called him the "Savior of Japan/Nissan" and "Mr. Fix-It"; they even made a whole manga series about him. Ghosn set an example of what *should* be done, and what could be accomplished if leaders are given the freedom to make the decisions that need to be made. He became the hero of Japan, achieving celebrity status.

Over the years, the automobile industry changed, and the general belief arose that there were too many manufacturers. Electric vehicles also gained in popularity, making it difficult for traditional automakers to compete. The solution, it seemed, was fewer automobile manufacturers so that those that existed would have a larger market and a better chance to be profitable.

Carlos Ghosn was a huge proponent of electric vehicles, such as Nissan's popular Leaf. He pushed the company to make more of them and criticized Nissan for not moving quickly enough in this space. The key components, structure, and construction process of the electric vehicle was much different than that of the internal combustion engine and would require completely different technology. A typical combustion engine car might have 30,000 parts, where a typical electric vehicle has fewer than half that number of parts. Ghosn, who was at this point Nissan's CEO, saw the industry's transformation coming. His vision and insight led him to forge deep alliances with other manufacturers including Renault in France and Mitsubishi in Japan. This was a trifecta of shareholding across the capital structures that would likely have helped Nissan retain its competitive advantage.

However, the Japanese government became curious about the arrangement. Other top management at Nissan, which was notoriously xenophobic, was raising red flags. They feared that Renault would take over Nissan, their sacred flagship, the "made in Japan" automaker. Even a merger would pollute the "pure blood" of the Japanese Nissan.

The Japanese government, in coordination with senior managers at Nissan, the police, courts, and even the media, were all in on a coup to take down the man that they perceived as a threat to their beloved automobile manufacturer. In November 2018, Ghosn, arriving in Japan from Lebanon by private jet, was promptly arrested and imprisoned. The country's public media organization, NHK, was conveniently present to cover the arrest.

That same month, Greg Kelly, a Nissan executive whom the Japanese government claimed was helping Ghosn carry out his "many crimes," was lured from his home in Tennessee to attend an important board meeting in Japan. The meeting was a ruse and like Ghosn, Kelly was also arrested. There were no concrete charges against him and no real evidence, but Kelly was still imprisoned for thirty-four days where his health issues were ignored, and he slept on the floor without heat in the dead of winter.[55] During that time, there was no clarity on when, if ever, he would get his freedom, let alone a "fair" trial—if such a thing is even possible in Japan. Indeed, "Abandon all hope, ye who enter Japanese courts," begins an article in *The Japan Times* about former judge Hiroshi Segi, who "grew so disenchanted with what he came to see is the 'corrupt' and 'ugly' realities of the nation's judicial system that after thirty years he quit his job and became a professor."[56]

55 Arcelia Martin, "'No Place Like Home': Ex-Nissan Exec Greg Kelly Returns after 3-Year Detainment in Japan," *The Tennessean*, March 14, 2022, https://www.tennessean.com/story/money/2022/03/14/greg-kelly-former-nissan-exec-ghosn-case-returns-nashville/7014405001/.

56 Tomohiro Osaki, "Ex-Judge Lifts Lid on Japan's 'Corrupt' Judicial System," *The Japan Times*, April 30, 2014, https://www.japantimes.co.jp/tag/hiroshi-segi/.

The original trial ended after three and a half years and a long string of human rights violations. He was found guilty of one of the charges and received a six-month suspended sentence. He is appealing the ruling but has finally been allowed to return to his family in the United States.

Kelly's US lawyer, Jamie Wareham, expressed their sentiment. "What a barbaric and disgusting turn of events," he declared. "First, they decided to destroy two Westerners to avoid tow failed Japanese companies (Nissan and Mitsubishi Motors) from becoming French. Then they tortured both Westerners for more than 150 days, and now they seek to regain inexorably lost face having had their asses handed to them at trial.[57]

Many charges were made against both Ghosn and Kelly, even though there was no legal process or even proof that either of the men had done anything wrong. Japanese officials had just decided they wanted to get rid of Ghosn because he was going to somehow give away Nissan to France, and it would no longer be a Japanese company. They now saw this man, who they had at one time admired as the savior of Nissan and Corporate Japan, as a foreign enemy leading the initiative to sell off the crown jewels to *gaijin*.[58]

They could have fired him, but they wanted to make an example of the man. They wanted to send the message, in their xenophobic way, that foreign managers are not welcome in Japan or at least are not given any real authority and/or credence. When then Japanese Prime Minister Abe was asked what

57 Roger Schreffler, "Former Nissan Executive Greg Kelly Sums up Ordeal," *Asia Times*, June 20, 2022, https://asiatimes.com/2022/06/former-nissan-executive-greg-kelly-sums-up-ordeal/.

58 *Merriam-Wester* defines "gaijin" as "a foreigner in Japan," https://www.merriam-webster.com/dictionary/gaijin.

he thought about the Nissan scandal, he said that it probably should have been resolved internally.

It *should* have been resolved internally—that was the smart decision. Making it public was terrible for the company. What was the real issue at stake? That Japanese companies are just that: Japanese and not to be touched by foreigners. The message Nissan sent to the Japanese and to the world was that foreigners should stay away. No one would be allowed to mess with Japan Incorporated.

JAPAN, INC.

In this book, the term Japan Incorporated, or Japan, Inc., follows this definition from The Free Dictionary from Farlex:

"Informal for the close relationship between the Japanese government and the private sector. The Japanese government guided private sector development following the Second World War, often using personal relationships between bureaucrats and executives rather than actual regulation. This term came to prominence in the 1980s and was used by Western businessmen. While some credit Japan Inc. with playing a major role in the Japanese miracle, others believe it led to corruption and contributed to the Asian financial crisis."[59]

Might there have been increasing friction between the "Japanese way of management" and the "foreigner's way of

---

59   *The Free Dictionary*, s.v. "Japan Inc," accessed June 11, 2022, https://financial-dictionary.thefreedictionary. com/Japan+Inc.

management?" Absolutely. But remember, the actions of that foreign management were what helped Nissan survive in the first place. Under Japanese management, the company was failing and about to go bankrupt. They brought in Ghosn, and he proceeded to hire more foreigners to add new perspective. Ultimately, that is what saved the business. Over the years, those frictions between management styles may have risen to the surface. Ghosn, with all his success, may have allowed his hubris and his pride to get in the way of his management process and decisions, rubbing others at Nissan the wrong way so to speak. That is entirely possible. Still, blaming Ghosn for whatever Nissan's executive management deemed to be a problem at the company doesn't hold water. This is a large public corporation with a board of directors and many senior managers.

As far as Greg Kelly's participation, everything we know about the man points to his innocence. Kelly was simply targeted as a foreigner and held as a sort of scapegoat. Where is the evidence that Kelly was involved in any wrongdoing at all at Nissan? *Asia Times* reported on the subsequent trial as follows:

> The fact that the presiding judge didn't toss the case out when he learned that Kelly's main accuser, Hari Nada, and one of the two lead outside lawyers advising Nada and other members of the coup, Hiroki Kobayashi of the firm Latham & Watkins LLP, had concealed exculpatory evidence speaks tons about the corruption of the Japanese criminal justice system and this case in particular.

> ...To be clear, if Kelly is found guilty, there is no guarantee he won't be tortured again. And, yes, he was tortured at the hands of his Japanese captors as were two other Americans, Mike and Peter Taylor, also "constituents" involved in the broader Carlos Ghosn case, as well as Ghosn himself...

...We've gone into detail about his experience—kept in solitary confinement for 34 days, to be exact, in the dead of winter in an unheated cell, initially without winter clothing. On a number of nights, temperatures fell into the 30s Fahrenheit.

Lights were on in his cell 24 hours per day. And during the day, when he wasn't being interrogated, he would have to sit in the corner, legs stretched forward and not allowed to stand up and walk around for exercise. On weekends and holidays, he was not allowed outside his cell for any "open-air" exercise.[60]

To understand how destructive and counter-intuitive Nissan's decisions were, think about how ridiculous the whole setup was. Even if there were nefarious activities—and there were some truth to what they were saying about Ghosn—the actions they claim he took could not be the fault of just one individual. The board would have known about these decisions. That's how it works. And if the board didn't know, then that points to a massive failure in corporate governance at Nissan that regulators should be investigating. Either way, if there were genuine wrongdoing, more people would have to be implicated in accusations of this size, and more people would have to be held accountable. You can't target one man in a public witchhunt. You need a careful internal review and examination to ensure the company is healthy.

But that is not what Nissan did. Instead, they chose the most destructive path, the *kamikaze* path—indeed, the "just-go-ballistic" path—in the attempt to send a message about the

---

60   Roger Schreffler, "Japan Has Tortured Three American Citizens," *Asia Times*, March 1, 2022 https://asiatimes.com/2022/03/japan-has-tortured-three-american-citizens/?amp_markup=1.

"real" owners of Japanese companies.[61] The real owners are not the shareholders or even the stakeholders, but rather the politicians, the elite, and the xenophobes. The message was clear: that Nissan is and always will be a Japanese automaker, and that anyone who believes differently is in danger of being locked up. That choice has been deeply damaging to the company. Their value has tanked. If you are an employee or senior management in a company, then that company doesn't belong to you: it belongs to its shareholders. In other words, in choosing the path of greatest destruction, you're damaging someone else's property. Will anyone be held liable for those decisions? We've seen another scandal at Toshiba, where they colluded with the Japanese government against foreign shareholders, again in secret and again with the consequence of eroding the company's value. There is a pattern here that needs to be addressed.

Recently, the United Nations came out with a report condemning Japan's handling of the situation, saying it was a massive abuse of human rights. The Human Rights Council Working Group of Arbitrary Detention called Ghosn's multiple arrests "fundamentally unfair," noting that he was arrested four times in a row to keep him detained. According to them: "The repeated arrest of Mr. Ghosn appears to be an abuse of process intended to ensure that he remained in custody. This revolving pattern of detention was an extrajudicial abuse of process that can have no legal basis under international law."[62] They intend to refer the case to the UN Special Rapporteur on

---

61 *Merriam-Wester* defines "kamikaze" as "having or showing reckless disregard for safety or personal welfare," https://www.merriam-webster.com/dictionary/kamikaze.

62 Hugo Miller, "Ghosn's Arrests Called 'Extrajudicial Abuse' by UN Panel," Bloomberg, November 23, 2020, https://www.bloomberg.com/news/articles/2020-11-23/ghosn-s-repeated-arrests-were-extrajudicial-abuse-says-un.

torture and other cruel, inhumane, or other degrading treatment or punishment.

The Japanese government responded that the United Nations was basically wrong in their assessment. By the way, the United Nations doesn't make idle claims. If they say there's a problem, there's a problem. They no doubt have substantial documentation and other evidence to support their assertion, and for an organization or entity to dismiss it is unsustainable behavior. For Japan's government to dismiss the UN is elitist and, in a way, feudalistic.

Claiming that the UN was wrong without providing any evidence to support that claim points to a pattern of behavior. Perpetrators are quick to turn around and say, *you're wrong*, but never actually provide any proof of that statement. This is what happened to me. The company just turned around and said, *you're lying*. This is what happens to women who complain about sexual harassment: the company says, *you're lying*. They gaslight and discredit you and then just move on, hoping no one will look closer. The Japanese government has yet to provide information on how the United Nations' assessment is incorrect.

This is the way Japan operates. It's actually a very authoritarian system, in some ways more so than perhaps a self-proclaimed communist state like China. The outside world doesn't see this about Japan, they only see what Japan wants them to see. In fact, in the 1980s, Japan developed the concept of "Cool Japan" which is an initiative to develop its cultural capital as a form of soft power. The Japanese government began funding TV shows like *Oshin* that showcased the Japan they wanted the world to see, while successfully distracting people from the issues they wanted to hide. It was essentially propaganda, similar to what you would find in authoritarian nations (and perhaps in Hollywood movies).

Ghosn probably wasn't trying to take away Nissan from Japan. He was likely looking out for the company's investors, acting in an ethical way that would have benefitted all stakeholders if his plan had been allowed to play out. We'll never know for sure though. Carlos Ghosn was placed in a Japanese detention center: a room with a cement floor, no bed, and with the lights left on twenty-four hours a day. Prisoners are given little food. It's literally torture. This is done to get prisoners to confess to something they may or may not have done.

Those who believe the Japanese legal system would save Ghosn would be wrong. Japan has a more than 99 percent conviction rate, thanks to the well-known collusion between judges and prosecutors. Judges have nothing but contempt for defendants, often calling them *yatsuda*, which translates as "those little bastards."[63] A story that is notorious in Japan is that of Iwao Hakamada. He was a convict who served five decades on death row before the judiciary realized he almost certainly didn't commit the crime. In *The Enigma of Japanese Power*, Dutch professor Karel van Wolferen writes that 63,204 people underwent their first criminal trial in 1968. Of that number, only 67 were acquitted.[64] If you were Ghosn, would you have any faith in a fair trial?

After six months, Ghosn was allowed out on $10 million bail. Not surprisingly, he quickly left the country and escaped to Lebanon. Obviously, he paid people to get him out of the country, but it does make you wonder. Ghosn was under 24/7 surveillance. Could he have really gotten out without them letting him? Perhaps the perpetrators knew that if Ghosn went

63   Hiroshi Segi, *Zetsubo no Saibansho* (Tokyo, Japan: Kodansha Ltd., 2014).

64   van Wolferen, *Enigma of Japanese Power*, 221.

to trial, more secrets would come out than they had bargained for, and they helped him escape.

There has never been a trial because Ghosn never returned to Japan. We'll never know if there was any truth to the charges. Ghosn claimed he was doing what Nissan had tasked him with when they made him CEO, help the company survive the coming transformation in the auto industry. Perhaps he was or perhaps he really did commit the crimes Nissan claimed. This is not a defense of Ghosn. But Nissan's and Japan's terrible handling of the situation—locking him up, trapping Greg Kelly, creating a public scandal, and committing human rights violations—makes him look very guilty. It was disingenuous, and certainly not a value-creating way of handling these issues.

With Ghosn out, Nissan's stock tanked. The company lost $6.3 billion in the year after the scandal, their first loss in eleven years. Yet, the Japanese government didn't seem to care about the profitability, or about the massive losses to shareholders and investors (not to mention stakeholders, employees, etc.). Their only concern, it seemed, was keeping Nissan in Japan, and making a "criminal" out of the very man they had elevated to "savior."

Regardless of who you believe in the matter of Japan versus Ghosn, this abuse of power negatively impacted investors. The story created a discount in the market for Japanese companies because potential investors see the country's companies as higher-risk investments. The power the government wields over corporations creates an unknown for potential investors. It's too unpredictable. The government's actions were not democratic or part of the capitalist equation, and investors entering a culture that presents so much uncertainty, as Japan does, are now more cautious about the money they're investing.

Corporate governance, discussed in the last chapter, affects many people, including investors. When that governance is corrupt from within or from without, investors' best interests are at high risk. Nissan's board of directors and senior leadership weren't considering their investors when they decided to oust Ghosn without a complete internal investigation, and with government and police assistance, as well as state-sponsored media coverage. In effect then, all stakeholders are beholden to the elite and/or to corrupt government officials.

All of that was unnecessary, and it destroyed the company. They must have known their actions would bring down the share price. If their suspicions about Ghosn were warranted, they could have dealt with the matter any number of ways that would not have impacted the stock negatively. They could have acted in a way that would have created value, increased the share price, and benefited shareholders. But word on the street is that the Deputy Prime Minister of Japan didn't like Ghosn. He is from an elite family with connections to the highest echelons of Japanese society. If there was a senior political figure with a grudge against Ghosn, it would certainly provide a reason for the government to try and get rid of him.

Disturbing as the Carlos Ghosn story is, it's not the first story of this kind we've heard from Japan. In the last chapter, we discussed Toshiba and how it colluded with the Japanese government to bully its shareholders. But more importantly, these are not only Japan's stories. They happen all over the world, with varying degrees of consequences. In Chapter 5, for example, we talked about how Mitsubishi bought 21 percent of Morgan Stanley with a $9 billion check. The reason they didn't buy Morgan Stanley *outright* is because the United States government wouldn't let them. Morgan Stanley was considered of critical importance to the American financial industry, and the United States government wouldn't allow a Japanese firm to own it. Similar protections are extended to American companies like Boeing, which are deemed "essential to national security." Japan may have displayed an extraordinary level of xenophobia and control when it came to Nissan, but similar incidents happen across the globe.

We can see that in the Great Financial Crisis. We talk about Japan a lot in this book because the examples are so blatant, and because it is what I'm familiar with. But more than a decade ago, a series of unsustainable behaviors originating in America brought the whole world to its knees and pushed us into a global recession. These stories about Toshiba and Nissan are so obviously unsustainable—both in the companies' actions and the government's denial—it's almost as if they assume Japanese citizens and shareholders are idiots. But how different is that from the Great Financial Crisis? The United States government and corporations pushed the global public right to the brink. They gave its citizens an ultimatum: "Either we use all your tax-payer money to save these huge corporations whose nefarious activities have got the world into this mess in the first place. Or, we wipe out all your savings in the banks. Which one would you prefer?" They also treated the public like idiots.

What is startling is how little we have learned from that crisis, and how little has changed. In *Too Big to Fail*, Andrew Ross Sorkin describes the Great Financial Crisis as "a chronicle of failure":

> ...It would be comforting to say that all the characters depicted in this book were able to cast aside their own concerns, whether petty or monumental, and join together to prevent the worst from happening. In some cases, they did. But as you'll see, in making their decisions, they were not immune to the fierce rivalries and power grabs that are part of the long-established cultures on Wall Street and in Washington.

In the end, this drama is a human one, a tale about the fallibility of people who thought they themselves were too big to fail.[65]

Replace Wall Street and Washington with Kasumigaseki, and you get examples like Nissan and Toshiba. Replace too big to fail with too big to care, and you have what we're describing in this book. The only way to break the cycle of failure, to stop embracing defeat, is to move to a more sustainable way of doing business. It is to adopt, for example, the UN's SDGs and implement sustainable profitability goals so that we can move back to that original aim of capitalism: generating outsized profits by adding extraordinary value to society (rather than causing net destruction of value to generate profits—*nefarious capitalism*).

INVESTORS' INTERESTS OVER TIME

Investors have always wanted a return on their money. That hasn't changed. If you're investing in a company that doesn't return a profit, you might as well donate to a nonprofit organization (NPO). Investors have a choice: they can hang onto their money and avoid risking potential loss of value, or they can invest it, which carries a risk, but also has upside potential. Smart investors always consider the risk involved in the potential of earning outsized returns. They want to put their money into solid investments that they can count on for long-term returns, not long shots that *could* pay off, yet have a high chance of losing value. Part of the risk assessment is determining the trustworthiness of a company in which they are investing. They need to trust those companies aren't engaged

---

65 Andrew Ross Sorkin, *Too Big to Fail: The Inside Story of How Wall Street and Washington Fought to Save the Financial System—and Themselves* (New York: Viking, 2009), 7.

in nefarious behavior that might put their money at risk, and they expect the company's decision makers to be good, honest people. It is the board's responsibility to choose top management and leaders who not only do things right, but also do the right things. That's the basic expectation.

The belief that you're trusting your money to the right people has always been central to an investor's decision to invest or not invest in a company. Honest businesspeople are transparent in their business dealings. They don't lie or cheat. They treat their employees well and don't, at least knowingly, cause damage to society or to the environment. Basically, the good and honest businessperson doesn't do anything that would cause the stock price or the value proposition to all stakeholders to go down. Investors don't give capital to a company so that they can spend it colluding with the government or lose it in nefarious dealings. They give it to them to grow. The whole premise is that capital will be multiplied, not destroyed, and value will be added to all stakeholders. Although admittedly, this can be a balancing act at times.

All of this has been true in the past and it is still true today, but there have been other changes in how investors evaluate companies. Around the late 1800s and early 1900s, people started asking questions, especially around issues like human rights and the environment. Investors wanted to know how companies treated their employees. They wanted to know whether they were using child labor or firing women who were pregnant. Later, they wanted to know what happened to the company's waste materials—were they reused, recycled, or properly disposed of? Or were they dumped into the ocean or a landfill, and were those waste materials then poisoning their neighbors or perhaps, inadvertently, themselves?

Those questions—and a greater demand for transparency—

have continued, and a hundred years later, investors want even more from corporations. They still want their returns, but they want them through vehicles such as ESG investing (or perhaps, more appropriately, GSE investing). They are looking for investment vehicles that aim to balance stakeholder needs and demands. In other words, investors want to know they're putting their money into businesses that have proper corporate governance, and that prioritize the environment and support society. They are seeking companies to invest in that make profits without marginalizing all stakeholders and they believe that adding value is not a zero sum game. It's not about stealing from employees to give to holders of capital. That, in fact, is socialism, or communism, as history shows us.

This is not anti-capitalism. Rather, it reflects capitalism's original intents and, in fact, the very heart of what capitalism stands for: making outsized profits while adding extraordinary value to society.

Businesses that have strayed from capitalism's original intent, yielding to, and often profiting from, the corruption of capitalism, are ripe for improvement through the correction mechanism of ESG. Of greater concern to these companies are the risks of not changing their ways. Eventually, a company that isn't ESG compliant won't only erode human rights or the environment—that erosion will be reflected in its stock price.

If a company is acting in nefarious ways, at some point the investment is going to go bad. Nissan's a good example of that: Things went bad, and shareholders lost money. They may have made a lot of money in the years leading up to Ghosn's arrest, but at the end of the day, they lost a lot of money due to poor corporate governance.

Corporate management and boards of directors are by definition responsible for minimizing risk and maximizing returns.

When they don't do it, they are not following their fiduciary duty. They are throwing away someone else's money, and it could be someone's pension, their life savings, or their very foundation for survival.

The Nissan example isn't an isolated case. Government intrusion into public investments is common in some countries. For example, a government might pressure a bank to offer high-risk loans to preferred entities, putting investors in that bank at risk of losing their own money. Yet Japan, operating under antidemocratic (authoritarian) principles, is known to do exactly that. Banks are a higher priority than shareholders. Regardless of what's best for investors, if the government directs a bank to make a bad loan, the bank makes the loan. This practice allows companies who behave inappropriately, like Nissan, to survive—they can get loans because the government forces banks to give them money.

Thankfully, investors have woken up to the fact that this type of corruption exists, and they are getting smarter about where they put their money. They see the impact that unethical governance has on their wallet, and they also see how it affects society. They want to make money, and they also want to know that their money is being used in an ethical way for the betterment of the world, not to support corruption. Investors are even willing to accept a lower rate of return if they are confident that their money is doing good in the world. They don't want to contribute to scandals. They don't want to support companies that imprison people without due process of the law. And at the end of the day, as we've seen, these "lower" returns may end up beating everybody when nefarious behaviors by "high-growth" companies like Nissan and Enron come to light.

In 1990, eight of the top ten largest companies in the world were Japanese corporations. Today, none are Japanese. In fact, in 2021, the largest Japanese company was Toyota, at #42 in the world. So what happened? The top companies by market cap are no longer in Japan. This is historical proof that bad behavior is unsustainable, and leads to not only a "brain drain," where the brightest talent and key people abandon companies and sometimes, countries, but also a capital drain on those countries that persist with these behaviors.

Investment has come full circle. At its early beginnings, people wanted to put their money in companies, products, and causes they believed in, but somewhere along the line that ideal became twisted, and the accumulation of wealth at any cost became the #1 goal. Investors still want to make money, but they realize that they can invest in highly profitable businesses that operate ethically, companies that they can be proud to support. ESG investing is part of this change, and it's bringing investors back in line with the true meaning of capitalism and supporting a circular economy. They want to put their money into enterprises that benefit them not only financially, but that benefit society as a whole in an ethical, sustainable way. They want to make sure that their capital is used in a way that results in benefits to all stakeholders.

This creates a circular protection system, and proliferation of "real value," where companies generate outsized profits but simultaneously add value to the environment, to employees, to women, to families, and to society. Families are the cornerstone of society and the future of healthy corporations and healthy economies. It's better than any insurance policy or legal department, and that's what ESG investors are looking for.

But there are still challenges ahead. Right now, there is no global standard for ESG compliance. There are different rating companies, like Yahoo Finance, Bloomberg, and Sustainalytics, but they use different metrics to calculate their ESG rankings, so it is difficult to understand what is being measured and what the differentiation factor is. There's no global system of evaluation. Investors who are looking to put their money in companies that are truly ESG compliant should do their own research, rather than rely on standardized scores. Similarly, companies should be upfront and clear about their ESG strategies—simply claiming "ESG" and putting it in a brochure is not enough. More research (from investors) and greater transparency (from companies) can push us all towards that goal of positive "real value creation," and a return to the heart of capitalism.

RISKS AND BENEFITS ASSOCIATED WITH HOW A COMPANY PRIORITIZES INVESTORS' INTERESTS

As with the risks of operating an enterprise that damages the environment, or society, or that practices unethical corporate governance, neglecting investors' best interests will cost a business dearly over time. Equity and debt capital will be more difficult to obtain, and unless the country steps in and forces a bank to lend money at a lower rate, doing business will cost more. Investors will sell off their shares and new investors will be wary and difficult to attract. The sustainability of the business will come into question, and with fewer investors and a higher cost of equity and overall cost of capital, they will eventually be unable to continue operations. Even if they are able to squeak by, competing with other businesses will become increasingly difficult.

This is where the correction mechanism really starts to take a bite. As more sustainability-focused investors continue to demand sustainability, companies that refuse to comply with that demand will have to rely on government bailouts, or they'll go under. Recently, TARP programs, bailouts, and other safety nets have been a huge disincentive for businesses to move in the right direction toward change that benefits all stakeholders and is sustainable. And unfortunately, everyone pays. Taxpayer dollars that could be used for much needed infrastructure improvements, schools, and other government-funded entities are short-changed as the money is directed to corporations. Rewarding people and corporations for nefarious actions is an expedient and efficient way to destroy value for everyone.

Companies that choose a path of sustainable business practices will attract investors and will be at a reduced risk of inviting scandals like those of Enron and Nissan. Their cost of capital will be less, providing more capital so they can compete with other businesses within their industries. Investors will be able to put their money into the company with confidence. ESG investing is a global trend that with standardized factors will make companies that follow these practices more attractive to people worldwide, improving their relations within foreign partnerships.

STRONG CAPITAL STRUCTURES

Ethical governance that benefits the investor also includes capital structure, which is part of the fiduciary duty of managers and boards of directors of a corporation. People who buy stock in a company expect to make a certain return, but if the company decides, for example, to hold a large percentage of their value in cash, they are not doing investors any favors. Investors expect the corporation to use its balance sheet to have a debt equity balance and to hold a minimum of cash in case of emergencies. That's it. Otherwise, they expect their capital to be deployed in business activities. Generally speaking, the concept is that the corporation exists to provide a service or to create a product, not to hold cash. Investors can hold cash on their own; they are the experts at asset allocation. The company's job is to do—to put out services and products with the purpose of mindfully and deliberatively adding value for stakeholders.

In other words, if a company holds a lot of cash, then they're trying to be investors instead of maximizing their raison d'être as an organization. Corporations hold cash in case of emergencies and possibly for M&A (mergers and acquisitions) opportunities, but you don't need a lot of cash on hand for M&A opportunities. You can go to your shareholders or to the market, make your case for the venture, and they will give you the capital if they believe in your proposition. And if they don't, you probably should reconsider your plans to move forward. If an organization keeps cash instead of using that money to generate value, then they are essentially saying they don't trust their shareholders, or that they can do a better job at asset allocation than their investors. They're not focusing on their core competencies, and that is inefficient and destructive to shareholder value.

All this comes down to what I call "sustainable balance sheet management," which is ensuring you have sustainable levels of debt/equity and that you maintain sustainable levels of investments. Excess cash is an example of how *not* to manage your balance sheet in a sustainable fashion. Cross shareholding, which we talk a little about in this book, is another example of poor, anti-capitalistic balance sheet management which is unsustainable.

HUMAN CAPITAL IS PART OF
THE CAPITAL STRUCTURE

The financial balance sheet of a corporation is part of the company's overall use of capital, which also includes the use of human capital. A manager who's focused simply on keeping their own job, in an effort to make themselves appear more valuable, can hire unskilled people who struggle by comparison. This is not a good use of human capital. A manager who instead hires people more educated, experienced, or skilled than themselves will add value to the business, despite perhaps putting their own job at risk. The hope is that leadership sees and appreciates this strategy and retains that manager, valuing their focus on the good of the company and their hiring skills.

VALUE OF DIVERSITY—WHO IS MOST QUALIFIED?

In any discussion of hiring, diversity must be acknowledged as an important part of the equation. In selecting members of a board, a company would do well to choose people who understand their business or a particular part of the business that company wants to improve. It might also make sense to bring on members from other industries with experience in a subject in which the current board is lacking and the company needs.

In addition to hiring, retaining employees is equally important. Companies that fire people who take family time are not using their human capital wisely. They spend a considerable amount of time and money vetting people to choose the most qualified. To then abandon them when they need to take a short-term leave for family is simply wasteful. It creates a loss of morale and productivity that will affect revenue and have ripple effects throughout the organization.

When I worked at Mitsubishi Morgan Stanley, a woman came up to me to say that she was leaving the company. I asked her a few questions about her reasons, and then I spoke to our colleagues, and it rapidly became clear she was leaving because she was pregnant. She was being harassed and pushed out. This woman was a phenomenal employee who brought tremendous value to the company. It is a classic example of short-term idiotic thinking, where you're punishing people for doing what they're meant to do as human beings. That's why you see virtually no women as CEOs in Japan, in the C-suite or even in management! In 2020, less than 8 percent of management roles were held by women, whereas the global average was 30 percent. At the end of the day, they get pushed out when they become pregnant, and you end up with a male-dominated, diversity-less senior management majority.

In contrast, respecting an employee's work/life balance improves efficiency and productivity. It attracts better talent and translates into better returns for investors.

While corporations have a fiduciary duty to investors, the onus is also on the investors themselves to invest wisely in companies that operate ethically and in the best interests of shareholders. People who simply follow investment trends (including ESG/SDGs), putting their money into the most popular companies with no due diligence, fail to take the full measure of a company's value. It is not enough to rely on ESG scores by different rating companies like Bloomberg and Yahoo Finance. These scores are based on different metrics, so it's difficult to know what exactly people mean when they say, "a company is ESG compliant."

The only way to learn a company's true value is through intensive research and hard data. Investors must talk to the employees and managers. They must have boots on the ground and investigate a company's returns, policies, and data. They should engage with management and use multiple data providers, core tools for setting a company's KPIs so they know when to invest in them—and sell when those KPIs are not met. They should know a company's corporate governance standards, its financial and human capital practices, its impact on the environment and society. Standardized ESG scores and rankings can be useful in the decision-making process, but they cannot be the sole criterion for investment; they must be part of a bottom-up investment selection procedure. Investors can be part of the problem or part of the solution.

KEY TAKEAWAY

Investors are becoming increasingly sophisticated, especially in regard to ESG and SDG concerns. The number of savvy investors is increasing, and the next generation will be even more concerned not only about profits, but about how a company operates and whether its operations are sustainable. The very definition of sustainability is being transformed. Corporations seeking long-term, high-quality investors should align their priorities accordingly.

GUIDED REFLECTIONS:

1. How have the questions that investors are asking you changed recently? What are their main concerns?

....

2. Are you attracting long-term, high-quality investors with real money? Why or why not? Consider ESG money, pension fund money, individual investors, etc. How much speculative investing is going on around your company?

....

3. How are you currently demonstrating to investors that your business is not only in the business of making outsized profits, but is also adding value to society?

....

4. Have you identified all of the key stakeholders in your enterprise? Have you analyzed the value proposition with each one?

....

5. Which of your key investors are you concerned might sell your stock, and where do you think they will be investing next? Why?

....

6. Have you done a strategic competitive analysis of capital allocation—in other words, the capital that's coming into your company from major investors? Investors are now changing the standards and criteria for their investment decisions, so what is your strategy to keep up, and get an outsized allocation of that capital for your company?

....

7. Are you managing your financial and human capital in a way that benefits investors?

....

8. How much cash do you hold on the balance sheet, and how do you explain that to investors?

....

9. What is your ROE (return on equity) and ROA (return on assets), and how do you explain that to investors?

....

10. When investors ask you about your priorities, how do you rank them in terms of customers, employees, and shareholders? Who comes first, and why?

....

11. What influence does the government have on your management's decisions?

....

12. Do you know what sustainable balance sheet management is? Please describe it here. If you don't understand what it means and you need help, you can call us at SVL, look it up, or search for help. But this is a concept that as a manager—and even as an employee—is important to understand.

....

CHAPTER 8

WORKFORCE

"It doesn't make sense to hire smart people and tell them what to do; we hire smart people so they can tell us what to do."

—STEVE JOBS

Sony was co-founded by Akio Morita after the Second World War. It was a very inventive and creative technology company that took off and had explosive growth until the eighties. The company grew large and became highly structured, regimented, and hierarchical in terms of Japanese business structure.

Employee wages followed a scale, where a new hire entered the company out of university at around twenty-five years old and was paid something like $20,000 a year. The next year wages increased to $21,000, then to $23,000 a year after that. Everyone made the same salary depending on how long they had been at the company, and everyone was a lifetime employee. Year after year, everybody got about the same bonus (plus or minus 5 percent), no matter how well or how poorly they performed. You might be the engineer who created the next multi-billion-dollar product, or the office worker who slacked off much of the day, and you both received the same pay and bonus. That was the typical, traditional, antimeritocratic, and thereby anti-capitalistic way of running a Japanese business, and it was how Sony was run.

Japan, by the way, has very poor intellectual property (IP) rights laws. The country also has a problem with the court system, as was noted in the Nissan story. They are basically kangaroo courts, part of a system controlled by large corporations and the government, with no regard for truth or justice. A company cannot rely on the courts to protect them, and they can't rely on IP laws to protect their intellectual property. You have to rely on your employees to be faithful and trustworthy. To be fair, historically, men basically became the property of their companies upon employment. Coupled with a pre-digital environment where IP theft would be more difficult, the risk—at least in the past—was quite low.

WEAK IP LAWS AND (MIS) APPROPRIATION IN JAPAN

Japan's unwillingness to protect intellectual property is echoed in the country's flagrant appropriation of IP from other countries and individuals. For hundreds of years, they have "borrowed" from other cultures and societies, "Japanized" the property, and kept it as its own.

They don't necessarily evolve the property either, but rather keep it intact. One example of this is *gagaku*, an ancient form of Chinese music that was brought to Japan hundreds of years ago. Today, it exists only in Japan, and in its original form. Author Donald Richie, commenting on Japan's habit of adopting the music of other cultures, noted that "Two hundred years from now, you'll be able to come to Japan and hear a perfect, original rendition of *The Beatles*' 'Hey, Jude.' That's probably the only place you'll be able to hear it."[66]

Copying a song may be innocent enough but copying the intellectual property of others can be quite damaging.

Not so long ago, foreign companies started to figure this out, and one of the first to capitalize on this weakness in the Japanese legal system was the Korean company LG. They recognized Sony's dominance in technology and the company's global success. They also saw the company's antiquated corporate system where people who added value to the business were shortchanged. LG saw a huge opportunity and they took advantage of it.

They acted immediately by poaching Sony engineers. LG looked at Sony's product line and went after the respective engineers for those products they wanted to duplicate. They focused on televisions for a while and hired clever headhunters to identify the key TV technology engineers at Sony. They discovered Sony's top talent and made them offers. A key engineer making $35,000 a year at Sony might be offered $1.5 million a year to work for LG, and LG would even move them and their whole family to Korea in the deal. They gave them guaranteed five-year contracts—enough money for an engineer to retire after a five-year stint.

Sony engineers were jumping at those bids. LG ended up with a lot of top talent that not only brought expertise, but

---

66 Donald Richie, personal communication with the author.

also brought Sony's intellectual property knowledge along with them. Sony could have offered their employees more money to stay, but they refused. To them, treating everyone the same was the same as treating everyone fairly. "We're not paying you more than $35,000 a year. If you want to go and work in Korea, you can go. We're Japanese and this is how we do things in our country. You get treated just like everybody else." Anyone who has lived and worked in Japan will have heard some version of this speech at one point. The assumption is that nobody is special, nobody is different, and nobody deserves a better bonus or more pay, no matter what value they bring to the company. Sony's engineers left in droves.

LG is now one of the most powerful television companies in the world. They're bigger than Sony in the TV business, and they basically bankrupted another competitor, Sharp.

Who is to blame for this transfer of talent from Sony to LG—from Japan to Korea? Sony could have paid their employees more money to stay. They could have paid people what they were worth instead of adhering to an antiquated system that rewarded underperformers and punished valuable employees. And this is only one example of many large, value-destroying policies that led to Sony's downfall. It's also the fault of Japan's laws that don't protect IP, and a court system that neglects to prosecute IP cases properly. In the end, pride and hubris cost Sony talent, money, and their place in the television business.

WORKFORCE TREATMENT OVER TIME

Lifetime employment wasn't originally intended to be a life sentence, or an exercise in selling your soul. People liked the job security that came with joining a company, a steady paycheck, and a pension to look forward to upon retirement.

This arrangement worked well until companies and employees took advantage of the situation. Businesses exploited lifetime employment by overworking their people and harassing them. Likewise, employees made the most of the situation by slacking off. It became a political game of staying out of the spotlight so that they could get away with as little work as possible. Clearly, the incentives were misplaced.

Not so long ago in Japan, if your resume listed more than one company, no one would consider hiring you. That attitude is gradually changing. If you have a couple of companies listed, there are some businesses that will consider you. But if you've worked for several different companies, and especially if you're older—say, over fifty—your employment chances are extremely slim, and if you're a woman on top of that, your prospects are nil.

In Japan, the tradition of job loyalty runs so deep that people get divorced over changing companies. If a husband comes home and says he lost or quit his job, it's not uncommon for the wife to take the children and leave, or for the husband to simply commit suicide.

This behavior grants corporations unearned power over their people, and many Japanese workers feel as though taking a job at a company is like agreeing to a life of slavery. This phenomenon is ingrained in Japan's culture. When a Japanese child begins their education, the school has to know where the child's father works. It's part of the entrance requirements. If the parent works at Mitsubishi, the child has a much higher chance of being allowed to attend the school than if, for example, the parent works at a convenience store. And if the parent loses his or her job at Mitsubishi, the child could find their days at the school cut short.

This culture causes all kinds of problems between employees and their leadership. A woman who is sexually abused by her boss is not going to say anything. It could not only cost her a career, but her children could be removed from school. She's trapped. The accompanying shame is also a factor that keeps workers in check. If you get fired from a good job and your neighbors find out, you could be shunned by them and even pressured to leave the neighborhood.

Fortunately, signs of change, even in Japan, are apparent. Younger people entering the workforce are less obedient to the antiquated rules, and their peers are more likely to support them instead of going along with the old ways. The world in general is moving toward better treatment of people in the workplace.

Not everyone is eager to move on, though. We're seeing a sort of division between the "sheep" and the "goats." Companies stuck in the past continue to mistreat their workforces, believing that they are so big that they can get away with anything. They think they're too big to care.

This isn't just a Japan issue; it's a global phenomenon. When my case came to light and was covered in the media, I had people reaching out to me from all over the world. A large percentage of those people were women, from the US, from Europe, from Canada, all of whom had been "restructured" because they were pregnant. There seems to be a feeling among larger corporations, internationally, that they can operate above the law. They have enormous workforces, they dominate markets, and they have the support of the government.

They are too big to care because they believe they are too big to fail. But that is not true. If you look at the top ten companies with the largest market cap from fifteen years ago, none of them are in the top ten today. Corporate "giants" don't last forever. Their size and power might continue to work in their favor for the time being, but it's not sustainable in the changing cultural environment.

In 2017, Toyota faced a huge scandal when one of their employees committed suicide due to workplace harassment. Bullying in Japan is a systemic problem, with corporations and society using harassment as a way to keep people in control. As van Wolferen states, it's also a way to keep citizens indoctrinated into Japan's way of functioning, what he calls "the System": "It [bullying] is a symbolic issue, with profound moral implications, between two camps struggling for control of the methods whereby upcoming new generations of Japanese adapt to the System."[67]

In the case of the Toyota employee, it was well-known he was facing extreme verbal abuse from his superior, but Toyota conducted an in-house investigation that determined there was no causal relationship between the suicide and the abuse. Two years later, in 2019, the Toyota Labor Standard Inspection Office determined that the employee had indeed taken his life because of the harassment, and his family was entitled to compensation. Toyota entered into settlement negotiations with the family. Four years after the event, in 2021, the president of Toyota personally apologized to the family and Toyota settled.

If you wanted to look at this positively, you could say that Toyota is moving in the right direction. After a death and four years of hell, the family finally received compensation. Toyota instituted a range of measures to protect against workplace harassment, such as a harassment hotline and a whistleblower protection program.[68] This is a big company, and they were forced to finally turn up at the ESG strategy table.

---

67 van Wolferen, *Enigma of Japanese Power*, 92.

68 Fumie Togami, "Toyota President Apologises Directly to the Bereaved Family, Reconciliation Young Employee Power Harassment Suicide," *The Mainichi*, June 7, 2021, https://mainichi.jp/english/articles/20210607/p2a/oom/obu/009000c.

But at the same time, how much has really changed? Toyota covered up the facts for as long as they could. When they realized they couldn't lie anymore, they came forward with a weak apology and offered measures that didn't have any real meat on the bones. We don't know if that hotline works or if that whistleblower protection program is any good. What happened to the superior who abused that employee? Was he fired, and if not, how was he dealt with? How are employees compensated? If there are third-party auditing parties, then how does that system work?

We don't have these answers because Toyota hasn't offered them. It hasn't been transparent about its actions. If potential employees of Toyota knew this story, would they be inspired to join the company? Or would they feel cautious about a business that tried to cover up workplace abuse that led to a suicide?

Companies that have moved forward, in a positive direction, look for ways to treat their people better. They know that workers are an extraordinarily valuable resource and the lifeblood of the business. These companies offer benefits and flexibility that allows people to work and still enjoy life outside of work. It's no surprise that these companies are having no trouble at all attracting the best and the brightest talent.

Newer companies in particular are more progressive, perhaps out of necessity. They don't have all the capital, the market, or other trappings that come with being an established brand. Some older companies are also beginning to catch on, especially in competitive capitalist countries. In countries with a lot of businesses and limited workforces, like the US, the UK, and others, companies have to work harder to attract the best people. Investors are interested in how these businesses treat their people, because they want to know that they're putting their money in a place that won't be riddled with scandals.

The increasing fluidity of the workforce should continue to

improve how companies treat their people. The best companies see employees as not only resources, but as people with lives of their own. They know their staff comprises individuals with interests and families outside of their jobs. They understand that talented people are not easily replaceable, and they have taken the strategic view that if they want a sustainable workforce, they have to be smarter about how they treat them.

There is no such thing as disposable human capital. People are precious and not to be taken for granted. If you shift your thinking from hiring people simply to achieve a short-term goal, such as the creation of a product, you miss the opportunity to nurture and develop a precious renewable resource that can benefit your business while enjoying their own individuality both inside and outside the corporation. This doesn't mean that people live forever—we know that's not true. But employees will be more likely to want to stay if they're valued throughout their employment. Again, thinking about the power of circles, seasoned staff with a wealth of knowledge and experience can mentor new ones, and new people can bring fresh ideas into a business, inspiring innovation.

People who have a good work experience tell their friends. They tell their families, write about it on online platforms like Glassdoor and Yelp, and sometimes encourage their children to apply for positions at the same company. In this way, the impact of a healthy workplace continues beyond an individual's retirement.

RISKS AND BENEFITS ASSOCIATED WITH HOW A COMPANY TREATS ITS WORKFORCE

Companies that stick to the old ways of taking employees for granted will find it difficult to bring on younger people. These later generations are less willing to work for companies that don't see them as human beings with lives outside of work. Businesses will create either a positive spiral of sustainability or a negative spiral to irrelevance with how they treat their workforce. The negative spiral leads to unhappy employees, more sick days, and decreased productivity. An attitude of apathy develops that spreads throughout the company, wiping out any passion people brought with them as eager and hopeful new recruits.

Low morale and low productivity affect product and service quality. It affects customer relations. It leads to employee turnover. Product quality is affected. Eventually, an unhappy workforce impacts the bottom line. In these types of environments, the best talent is the first to go. They have options and can be selective, so they will seek out other opportunities where they're valued and treated well. The worst employees will be the last to jump ship and may never leave. They're willing to put up with the poor treatment as long as they have a job.

These hangers-on are eventually promoted into managerial positions where they continue the legacy of controlling, rather than motivating, the workforce. Imagine a person working in this environment for years becoming a manager and then being tasked with bringing on new talent. How likely are they to hire people who are creative or who can think for themselves? If given the choice to hire a person with fresh ideas or one who will toe the line, which person are they most likely to welcome to the company?

You can see how the negative spiral continues with no one around to slow it or move it in the opposite direction. As Steve Jobs famously said, previously quoted at the opening to this chapter, "It doesn't make sense to hire smart people and tell them what to do; we hire smart people so they can tell us what to do." Good companies hire good talent and leave them to their own devices. But you can't encourage that culture if you have a series of bad managers hiring people who only want to follow orders. This is not a sustainable business practice.

A company intent on building the foundation for a multi-generational, global company that's on track to achieve exponential growth is not populated by obedient followers of an ancient protocol. It's looking to hire the next generation of bright, educated, passionate people who want to work for a company they believe in, and that believes in them. Younger people may be more likely to change jobs than their predecessors were, but they will be less likely to move on if they're in a place that makes them happy, at work and at home.

The woman who is pregnant and knows that after she takes time off to have her baby she will return to her current role will have more peace of mind. The man whose child is sick and needs to make weekly trips to a specialist will know he can take his son for treatments without worrying about losing his job. He will breathe easier. He will in turn be more loyal and perform better on the job.

Companies spend incredible amounts of money recruiting people. During my time at Mitsubishi Morgan Stanley, I flew all over the world—from Japan to Hong Kong, London, Boston, San Francisco—to meet with new college graduates and other candidates for positions with the company. The company spent a lot of money on those trips, and more paying people to screen the candidates and interview them. People went through round after round of interviews, and those who were being considered were flown to the head offices in New York, Tokyo, London, or Hong Kong.

By the time the right person is selected and offered a job, more than a hundred thousand dollars have been invested. This is common practice at many large companies. Yet once that educated, intelligent person that the company has invested so much time vetting enters the company, they're at the mercy of a manager who sees the person as just another resource to be used up. That person could be mistreated, harassed, or even fired based on some manager's outdated leadership practices.

The financial impact of hiring people only to chase them away goes beyond the initial investment. The person who leaves has also cost the company in onboarding, training, and setting up their workspace. The person, if they leave, takes intellectual property gained or developed by them, too, and depending on the country they're in, protecting that IP may be difficult for the company. The person will no doubt share his or her experiences with friends, family, and perhaps even on social media and websites like Glassdoor, discouraging other people to work for that company. Word will leak out in the marketplace.

One of the top financial headhunters in Tokyo once told me that he routinely advises his clients to steer clear of jobs at Mitsubishi Morgan Stanley. "It's not the salaries," he said. "Those are competitive with the rest of the industry. It's the corporate culture. I have heard so many horror stories from people who I've placed there that now I never recommend the company to anyone. To be honest, my only clients who are connected with Mitsubishi Morgan Stanley are people desperately trying to leave who beg me to find them jobs elsewhere."

Businesses that treat people shoddily make it very easy for the competition. All they have to do to attract top talent is simply treat people better.

Smart companies hire the best and the brightest, people with great ideas who will bring those ideas to the company. Those companies allow people the freedom to express themselves freely, communicating their ideas and collaborating with other bright people to create better products, better services, and better ways of running the business. They don't want these bright people to simply follow orders. When you allow really bright people from very diverse backgrounds to influence the ideas, culture, and development of your corporation, you've found the sweet spot.

If you want to know how you're doing with your workforce, ask them. Provide anonymous surveys for them to complete. Ask them what they like and don't like about working for the company. Ask them what they think the company could do better. You should have a third-party organization conduct this independent research so that employees can be honest without fear of the repercussions. It is crucial that your workforce trust the impartiality and anonymity of the survey, and that is difficult to ensure if it is run internally. Likewise, you should be able to trust the third party to discover what your employees really think, and what the company's systematic and cultural issues are.

You also need to be committed to change. You should have whistleblower protection programs in place to safeguard those who speak out, and policies to deal with perpetrators and problems. Otherwise, your survey will be considered another "trap"—like those toll-free company numbers for complaints—and you won't ever learn what your people really think and how your company can be better.

Exit interviews are another source of information, though most companies seem to do them poorly. Once a person's given their notice, companies may be eager to get them out the door. Instead, you should find out why they're leaving. Taking the job in the first place was a major decision—what made them change their mind? These interviews are even more important than entrance interviews in terms of understanding your company's culture. They're an opportunity to discover what's going on that you're not seeing.

A manager isn't likely to call attention to a problem they have in their own department. It makes them look bad. The only way to learn about workforce issues is to ask the workforce itself. Think of it this way: If you search the world for that perfect diamond, you find it and put it in your pocket, then one day you realize it's fallen out of your pocket, would you just keep walking? Or would you turn around and try to find out where you dropped it? And wouldn't you do something about that pocket? If you don't figure out where that diamond went, you wasted a lot of time and money seeking it in the first place. And if you keep walking around in those same pants, you're going to lose a lot more diamonds.

Of course, you have to hire well to begin with. If you've done that, you'll have fewer exit interviews. When someone leaves, ask yourself, "Were they presented with enough opportunities to achieve their career goals?"

You can work with your HR department to develop the right questions to ask a person in an exit interview. Their report should list who the person's manager was, and anyone else they reported to, so you can look for trends. If you're losing a lot of people under certain management, you could have a problem with that manager. They may need training. You will also want to know how the person who is leaving was treated and why they are leaving. When they came to the company, they had certain expectations. Which ones were met, and which were not? Why? What could the company do differently that might have made them stay? The exit interview is perhaps the most critical resource you have for identifying problems and creating an environment that promotes a satisfied, passionate workforce. You want staff members who believe in your company and share its goals. People who want to work for you and are eager to spread the good news about your business. People who are raving fans of their employer—your business!

KEY TAKEAWAY

People are indeed the lifeblood of any company. They are the source of ideas and innovation. They can bring passion and commitment, or apathy. Their attitudes are affected by the environment the company creates for them. The relationship between company and employee is symbiotic, and it develops over time. Everyone you hire becomes part of your corporate ecosystem, and if it isn't sustainable, that ecosystem will kill the company.

GUIDED REFLECTIONS:

1. Of the people you've hired, how many stay beyond five or ten years?

    ....

2. For those who have stayed, why are they still with the company? Why did others leave?

    ....

3. How much did those who left cost the company to hire and train? How much have you invested so far in those who have stayed, and what are you doing to keep them?

    ....

4. Did you have a conversation with the last person who left your company?

    ....

5. When you walk around the company, do people make eye contact or do they avoid interacting with you? What do you see in their faces? What does the atmosphere feel like to you? Are people enthusiastic and excited to come to work, or are they going through the motions? Do they bring their ideas to you, or do they feel like they have to keep their ideas to themselves and just do as they are told?

....

6. Why do people join your company in the first place? What do they hope to gain, and are you making promises that you can and are willing to deliver?

....

7. Would you want your sons and daughters or other family members to work for your company?

....

8. Are you developing leaders in your organization?

....

9. Have you created room in your company for leaders, or do you only have space for managers?

....

10. Do you conduct anonymous surveys to find out what your workforce thinks? If you do, are these surveys conducted by third-party evaluation companies? What measures do you have in place to act on what you learn, and do you have whistleblower protection programs to safeguard those who speak out?

....

CHAPTER 9

CUSTOMERS

"Do what you do so well that they will want to see it again and bring their friends."

—WALT DISNEY

At the company where I worked, the woman in charge of customer-facing business in Singapore was very popular with clients. In particular, she had developed strong long-term relationships with our key customers. They loved her, and it showed in her sales.

One day the woman began experiencing health problems. She went to her doctor and found out she had a tumor in her throat. It was cancerous and had to be removed immediately. She spoke with the senior management at Mitsubishi Morgan Stanley in Japan and was assured that she could take time off for the surgery.

Three weeks later, she was back at work—and was promptly fired. There was no official reason given. In management's eyes, she had committed treason and no further explanation was required. This happened over a decade ago, and the company still hasn't been able to win back the business they lost over that move. This wasn't a trivial amount of business either—she had major clients, and they were loyal to her, not the company. When they learned how she had been treated, they took their business elsewhere.

Consider the alternative: The company could have done the right thing and given the woman time off for the surgery and extra time to recover. They could have assured her, her teammates, and her customers that she would be taken care of and appreciated. They could have sent her flowers or some other gift. They could have decorated her office and welcomed her back with open arms. Indeed, that's what they say they do on their website. They claim that "it is essential that female employees play an even more active role" in the organization, and that they've introduced "initiatives" including "back-to-work seminars for employees on childcare leave."[69] This employee didn't get a "back-to-work" seminar; she got fired. But imagine if the company had acted in line with its claims. How would that story have played out with their customers?

It's not just this company—misogyny runs rampant throughout the Japanese system and many systems throughout our world. There was a scandal a few years back about medical schools. Japan has a high percentage of male doctors, and they discovered this was because medical schools were setting the entry bar higher for women, making it difficult for women to join the profession.

Recently, they discovered the same thing was happening in Japanese high schools: in 80 percent of Tokyo high schools, girls needed higher marks than boys to qualify.[70] In other words, there's

---

69 Towards a Better Working Environment," Mitsubishi Morgan Stanley, accessed January 31, 2023, https://www.sc.mufg.jp/english/company/sustainability/employee_environment.html.

70 Akira Okubo, "Girls Still Need Higher Entrance Exam Scores than Boys at 80 Percent of Tokyo High Schools," *The Mainichi*, May 26, 2021, https://mainichi.jp/english/articles/20210526/p2a/oom/ona/017000c.

a lot of talk about promoting women but the system is designed to restrict access to the top. Whether it's management, politicians, or senior leaders, they're specifically—by their decisions, regulations, and policies—keeping those top positions reserved for men. See Figure 9.1 for the world ranking of women in leadership.

WORLD RANKING OF WOMEN IN LEADERSHIP

Japan Ranks **Worst** in the G7 and 121st in the World

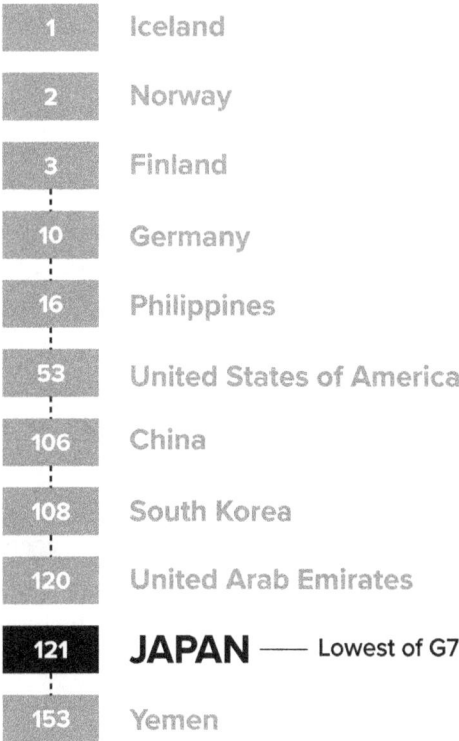

1	Iceland
2	Norway
3	Finland
10	Germany
16	Philippines
53	United States of America
106	China
108	South Korea
120	United Arab Emirates
121	**JAPAN** —— Lowest of G7
153	Yemen

Figure 9.1

It's not too much of a stretch to say that every dollar spent to make that employee happy would have resulted in thousands of dollars of business—maybe tens or even hundreds of thousands. But in the end, the company lost the goodwill of their clients, they lost a whole lot of money, and they lost an excellent representative of the company.

In fact, this shouldn't count as value lost, but as value destroyed. These actions affect the bottom line. It should be calculated in the profit and loss of the team and of the organization. Get HR involved; put a spreadsheet together. How much was lost not only in terms of the value and profit this employee generated, but also in terms of clients who will no longer do business with the company? Calculate it not just for this year, but for the next ten years—because that's the ripple effect of these actions. Maybe then someone will stop to measure the magnitude of the loss generated by bad management practices. Maybe then they'll assign that loss—mark to market on balance sheets and raised in performance reviews—to these managers who make these decisions. Because without this accountability process, this cycle of destruction is just going to continue.

Best practice would be to have these measurement processes and due diligence in place *before* the firing happens; the company should know the value they're giving away before their employee is out the door. We talk a little more about this in the management chapter, but what these managers are doing when they take these vindictive firing decisions is essentially "ruling by fear." They're attempting to assert their power in the most childish way possible. It's a sign of a weak leader—and it's costing the organization dearly. So let HR put those costs down in real numbers, so that you understand the full impact of letting a manager fire a great employee because they got cancer or because they became pregnant. Look at what you forfeit in terms of business, hard cash, brand image, loyalty, and customers.

You should never make the mistake of assuming that the way you treat your employees won't impact your customer relationships. Customers are watching and they're aware when the person they're working with—the salesperson, support person, or any other customer-facing employee—isn't happy in their job. That information may be public too, and customers are watching and making buying decisions based on what they hear and read about how a company treats its people. All employees are in some way "customer facing." They need to be fanatics for your business. Then you won't simply have employees and customers—you'll have "raving fans"—and that is where the magic begins.

Likewise, leaders should be just as discriminating about who they do business with—their partners and their customers. The people you choose to do business with reflects on you and your company and can affect other's decisions about working with you.

If you're building a sustainable company, one that makes outsized profits while adding extraordinary value to society, yet your customers are on a different path, ask yourself whether those are the best customers for your business. Customers that aren't committed to sustainability may, themselves, not be around for the long haul. Is it worth your time to build relationships with customers who are either unaware or unconcerned about your business practices regarding governance, society, and the environment? The lifecycle of those customer relationships may only be short term. Wouldn't your time be better spent cultivating long-term relationships with customers who are more likely to stick around?

Remember, SDG and ESG aren't simply acronyms meant to

satisfy some governmental agency or placate the public. They are the foundation upon which you can and should develop goals and initiatives to ensure steady, long-term, capital success that includes both profitability and value to society. The days of companies paying lip service to CSR (Corporate Social Responsibility), of promoting it so that they could put it in their fancy brochures and hand it out at board meetings to their investors as opiates of the people—those days are relics of the past.

I'm not suggesting you dump every customer that isn't on your same path. I am saying that you should see this as an opportunity to educate them. Open the dialog—start that conversation. See whether they are amenable to learning more and supporting your sustainable goals, as well as your product. After all, business is all about relationships.

CUSTOMER RELATIONSHIP MANAGEMENT HAS CHANGED OVER TIME

In the past, customers were less concerned with how a company operated. They didn't care to know how a business treated their employees, or impacted the environment, or whether it practiced ethical and transparent corporate governance. Today, people are much more aware of these factors and are influenced by them in their purchasing decisions. The movement toward Sustainable Development Goals and environmental, social, and governance criteria promises to continue to bring attention to matters of sustainability, the environment, and society. An evolution in how people buy, and how they choose which companies to work with, is unfolding.

This movement of social responsibility that began in the 1960s has finally been embraced by the majority of the public and by many corporations. Although some businesses still believe they can satisfy expectations by making donations of time and money to good causes, others have grasped the need to do more.

A business that doesn't have an SDG strategy or doesn't abide by sustainability criteria and just makes donations is disingenuous. Planting a hundred trees in your city doesn't make up for a thousand trees your company destroyed in the rainforest. Customers want companies to change the way they operate. They want new, real sustainable goals to be ingrained in a company's mission and to be an integral part of how it does business.

Unfortunately, so many bad actions are covered up. Whenever there's an oil spill or a nuclear plant meltdown, the whole world knows about it, as they should. Yet, Japan continues to dump nuclear waste into the ocean and no one's paying attention. Why isn't the United Nations up in arms? Who is Japan paying to keep quiet? Why doesn't the media report it? All you have to do is look at a radiograph to see the impact of the dumping flow around the world's oceans.

Recently, companies have made changes that were a very long time coming. Take for example the racist marketing and images for American products like Aunt Jemima's Syrup and Uncle Ben's Rice, brands that were successful for the companies they represented years ago, but are highly offensive to today's Black community. Or the negative "slur" terminology and imagery in reference to Indigenous People in the branding of sports teams, such as American baseball's Cleveland Indians (now the Cleveland Guardians) and the Atlanta Braves. People have been offended by the use of African American and Native American imagery for many years, yet it took public outrage and courageous, strong voices to wake many business up to the fact that people cared about how their values aligned with, or were at odds with, those of the customer.

Over the years, popular management philosophy has shifted from pure authoritarianism to a mix of more collaborative, engaging, communicative, and open management styles, among others. Management best practices have been almost exhaustively researched, and we have a plethora of incredible resources on the subject at our fingertips. These are quickly becoming global best practices and the prerequisite and the cornerstone for business and corporate management. In other words, good management practices aren't really a secret. Some people may be better leaders than others, but the basics of good management have been known for a long time—we shouldn't be wondering at this point what they are. But if we know them, and we aren't practicing them, then maybe we don't have the right managers.

The 1990s turned the focus toward environmentalism and health. Tobacco companies and junk-food manufacturers were highly scrutinized, and there was a rise in lawsuits over public health and the ramifications of their products. Oil companies, chemical companies, and other corporations soon came under scrutiny. The current century has seen the proliferation of cybercrimes, privacy issues, identity theft, data breaches, and other digital invasions that raise ethical issues around how much information a company should be able to collect, sell, and share with other companies.

The quandary for business is how to collect, analyze, and utilize big data to better serve customers without invading their privacy or opening them up to identity theft. Customers want to be better served, but they don't want their personal information shared with third parties. They want it protected, and they don't want their data mined without them knowing. This presents a dichotomy for companies that want to do the right thing for their business and their customers, and many are still struggling to find the right balance.

Companies are closer to their customers than ever before. They realize that customers are people with values and opinions, and if they feel a business isn't aligned with their own values, they will let them know about it. This is why companies have prioritized knowing more about their customers than ever before.

KNOW YOUR CUSTOMER

In many business sectors, opportunities exist for companies to take advantage of their customers. Laws that protect the consumer evolve over time, often due to events that have proven catastrophic for the customer and created the urgency required to make these kinds of laws a priority.

The term "KYC," or "know your customer," refers to several customer relationship concepts included in finance and fiduciary duties. For example, if you don't know the risk tolerance of your customer, then you won't know which financial products to offer them. The SEC developed rules such that once a finance professional has a risk tolerance definition for a client, it's illegal for the advisor to offer that client a product beyond their tolerance. If, for example, their risk score is three and you offer them a product with a risk score of five, you are open to disciplinary actions.

Here is why risk tolerance scores and enforcing them is important: Say the customer is a retired couple living on 401(k) money or other retirement funds. A financial advisor who doesn't comply with their fiduciary duty might offer the couple a derivative strategy that could pay off well, but the unlimited downside of the investment could wipe out their entire retirement fund overnight. That advisor is bound by regulations to not take that risk.

Another part of KYC addresses money laundering, Ponzi schemes, drug running, and other activities that involve illegal financial transactions. A professional in the finance world has to do their due diligence to know their prospect before they accept them as a customer. They have to ask a lot of questions: Where do you live? What is the source of your wealth or income? How many homes do you own and where are they located? What types of transactions are you planning to do, how many, and how often?

The answers can be quite revealing, and a professional advisor should have a method for assigning a score to the answers that determines whether the prospect is a good candidate for becoming a client.

These rules apply to any customer relationship, in any sector or business, to a greater or lesser degree. Today, "Know Your Customer" has exploded, and there has been a complete revolution in terms of what the concept means. In the old days, most businesses had client relationship management tools that allowed them to develop a file of information about each customer, so they could better serve them by offering products that meet their needs. This is still the case, but it has been taken to a whole new level with artificial intelligence and Big Data. Product development, company strategy, outreach—all of it is based on KYC. Entrepreneurs are even buying data from Amazon to see if their start-up ideas are viable. If the data says no, they don't begin the ventures. KYC is shaping our current business landscape and directing its evolution.

In every business, there is a lifecycle associated with each customer that helps predict their needs. As the servicer of a client, it's up to you to forecast those needs before the client does. This is a common practice in finance that applies in other sectors. Customer acceptance policies, customer identification, monitoring customer transactions, and risk management apply in virtually all businesses, and with all customers. And if it doesn't apply to everyone today, it will tomorrow.

Building sustainable relationships with customers is profitable, but knowing your customer goes beyond making money. It assists with managing supply and demand, knowing your customer's situation over time, and identifying trends that help you plan for their future. You need more information, such as your customer's goals and what they expect from their relationship with a company. As Steve Jobs said, "Get closer than ever to your customers. So close that you tell them what they need well before they realize it themselves."

Companies that gather a lot of information about customers have a responsibility to protect it. Compliance laws and cybersecurity have expanded over the years, in part due to the ease by which third parties have hacked into company databases. Ultimately, relationships between clients and companies that collect large amounts of data are mutual trust relationships. There's an Alexa or Siri in almost every home now, and their access to our data is unprecedented. If, say, a company like Amazon starts slipping up and there are data breaches, a customer's trust in the company would be broken and it would severely impact Amazon's profits and growth—perhaps even its survival. In other words, these relationships need mutual trust to survive. Companies like Apple are recognizing this; Apple released a whole wave of ads about how their data privacy systems are the best.[71] Their message was clear: if you care about who gets to keep and track your data, choose Apple.

Another side of KYC that we hear less about is KYB, or

71   apfelspot, "iPhone—Online Ad—Privacy Over Sharing (Updated with iPhone 12)," YouTube video, 0:15, February 21, 2021, https://www.youtube.com/watch?v=4Ri5yktl6GY.

"know your business." A person in business needs to understand exactly what business they're in. What may seem obvious isn't always what you may think. These questions should be answered by leadership and codified so that all employees understand the job and their role in it.

MORE THAN CUSTOMER SATISFACTION

Meeting a customer's wants and needs isn't enough. Customers expect corporate responsibility. They want to know where the resources come from that are used to develop the product, and how it's made. They want to know if a company has sustainable, environmentally friendly, socially conscious practices.

Customers are looking at tags to see where clothing is made. They may like getting shirts at cheap prices at big box stores, but are they okay with wearing a shirt that was sewed by children at a labor camp in Bangladesh?

The internet, and social media in particular, have made it much more difficult for businesses to hide bad practices. If customers aren't happy, the world will hear about it. This can be intimidating for a business that's worried about being "found out," but you want to hear people's opinions. You want to know what they approve of, and what you're doing that's preventing them from becoming a customer.

Comments on your website or social media can tell you whether you're going after the wrong customers or if you have a problem with your business, your product, or your services. If customers aren't happy, find out why and take action to fix the problem. Are you pursuing the wrong customers? Are your company practices at fault? Is your marketing off base? The worst thing a company can do is ignore customer complaints. They won't go away, and in fact they will only get louder.

The idea of the CEO in the corner office is quickly waning. Today's CEO is more connected to their company, their employees, and their customers. That old-time corporate structure of the boss sitting on the throne and reigning over the kingdom went out of style years ago. Today's leadership could better be defined as mindful servant leadership. Good leaders don't act like their people are here to serve them. Rather, they work to serve their people, be they employees, customers, or shareholders.

Servant leadership is not a new concept and, to be honest, it's not that hard. All leaders have to do is believe in their people. They have to put aside their egos and trust them. And they have to learn what motivates their people, because it may not be the same thing as what motivates them. Plus, if leaders *like* their people, then their job is infinitely easier. So many of the problems of bad management come from this essential dislike and distrust in employees, and an inability to let go of control.

Bad managers think they must be king, or they're not managers at all. Good leaders know better. If you don't let go of your ego, and if you aren't willing to work with your people at their level, then your job is going to be hard. But if you put aside your need for control, believe in your employees, and motivate them, then your leadership can move mountains. Those leaders who have done this, and who have done it well, have been very successful.

An excellent example of a CEO who understood this concept is the recently passed Tony Hsieh. I met him a number of times, and though we weren't close enough for me to claim him as a friend, he was extremely likable. I wish I had known him better.

Hsieh started Zappos, and though he was worth hundreds of millions of dollars, he lived in a trailer park. He liked his life and refused to change it simply because he had a lot of money. Hsieh wanted to set an example as the CEO of Zappos, showing his people that he and they were all part of the same team. He also believed in taking great care of Zappos's customers. When shoes started being sold online, Hsieh came up with a new model where a customer could choose several pairs and have them delivered. They could keep the ones they liked, then ship the rest back to Zappos for free. Amazon was so impressed with the Zappos model that they tried numerous times to buy the company.

Hsieh had a deep understanding of who Zappos's customers were. He knew what they wanted, and he figured out how to deliver it so well that his customers didn't want to buy shoes anywhere else. He knew that a happy customer keeps coming back, and Zappos customers were so happy that they couldn't stop talking about the shoes and the experience of being a Zappos customer. Hsieh built real relationships with his customers that would sustain the business long past his departure in 2020 and his reported untimely death.

Likewise, there's a reason people have favorite restaurants. They love the food, the atmosphere, and the service. A restaurant that delivers on those three fronts can charge a little more and people will still keep coming back for the experience. That's sustainability.

By building an increasingly satisfied, continuously growing customer base, you will have more loyal customers than you will know what to do with. This is the circular relationship that you want to have with your customers. You serve them well and they return the favor with loyalty, and by referring others to your business. This way, you create fans, not customers. You don't see them as a single transaction, but as long-term relationships that make your business sustainable and help it grow.

How a company behaves also has an enormous impact on customer loyalty. When the Great Financial Crisis hit and several companies were being rescued from bankruptcy by the government, Ford was offered a similar bail-out package. They refused. It was a difficult decision for the company to make, but it earned them many loyal fans. The Great Financial Crisis was more than a decade ago now and there are still people who will only buy Ford cars. To them, Ford was one of the few American companies that didn't take taxpayer money to stay afloat, and that meant Ford deserved their loyalty and respect.

RISKS AND BENEFITS OF CUSTOMER EXPERIENCE STRATEGIES

In Japan, *Tono Sama Shobai* (kanji: 殿様商売) refers to the old way of doing business with an antiquated attitude: "I'm the owner of a fantastic company with a fantastic product. You as the customer are privileged to buy my product, so give me your money and be grateful that I allow you to be my customer." Believe it or not, companies still exist that treat customers this way.

Some of those businesses are so big, or are supported by governments, or have such a monopoly over their markets, that they'll survive for a while. Some stay in business under the protection of their governments. But many are ripe for disruption. In Japan, startup banks are beginning to give institutions like Mitsubishi Bank some competition. The convenience store 7-Eleven has financial services terminals in their network of stores, an option that's gaining in popularity.

Other companies are allowed to stay in business despite their poor treatment of customers due to what's known as "cross shareholding." In this strategy, businesses exchange shares with their key business customers, effectively becoming major shareholders in each other's businesses. This way, their capital structures are locked together, and one company can treat the other poorly without risk of losing them as a customer. They also lock-up the shares in their "network" to avoid takeovers. In this way they force their way through the gates of "sustainability" by sidelining capitalism. This practice will also not be long-lived. This is fake sustainability and false stability in our global world of choices and increasing transparency.

Cross shareholding is historically a popular structure in Japan, so companies are less likely to make changes. It's basically a temporary measure to delay the inevitable—irrelevance. Cross shareholding was promoted by the Japanese government, especially after the Second World War, when stability was the foremost priority. The government wanted full lifetime employment of the country's workforce and no corporate bankruptcies. This method helped the country at a critical time in history. However, the practice has outlived its usefulness, and is now a throwback to the past that has no place in the modern business structure. Unless, of course, socialism and protecting the old guard elite is the top priority?

There are, of course, countries like this, where protecting the interests of the elite is more important than GDP, than consumption, than building infrastructure or helping the majority of your citizens. In many ways, Japan is like this. Cross shareholding is the tip of the iceberg, as we've seen. You've got a shrinking economy and a shrinking demographic but an elite that's growing more powerful. You've got governments colluding with businesses, as in the recent Toshiba scandal. If you see a structure where a monopoly is held up by government support, where companies are locked in relationships like cross shareholding that maintain the status quo—no matter how destructive that status quo is—then those are very clear warning signs of an unsustainable system of management. Beware. These are scandalous relationships that perpetuate a destruction of value and a continuous shifting of wealth to the elite. The downside of these tactics is a loss of creativity. Employees aren't happy, and that affects the happiness of society. This equates to less innovation, slow growth, and fewer products. As the world globalizes, companies that rely on government protection and cross shareholding lose their competitiveness in the market. Companies that don't enjoy oligopoly protection or don't have an impenetrable monopoly, yet continue to do business the old way, will eventually die out. The demise of these businesses won't happen overnight, but the competition will slowly chip away at market share, or they may be disrupted more suddenly. Time will tell.

The goal of progressive, customer-focused businesses is turning customers into fans. If you don't know the difference, look at Apple users versus Windows users. Microsoft Windows customers use the platform because they have to—it's what their workplace gives them. Apple users stand in line for hours waiting for their chance to buy a new product because they love the company, the brand, and the product. Create a fan base and you've created an unstoppable business model.

"There is a profound difference between management and leadership, and both are important. To manage means to bring about, to accomplish, to have charge of or responsibility for, to conduct. Leading is influencing, guiding in a direction, course, action, opinion. The distinction is crucial."

—WARREN BENNIS

KEY TAKEAWAY

A company that is willing to really know the customer, understand their needs, and develop a relationship with the customer can turn that customer into a fan. From there, the upside is unlimited. That customer will keep coming back for every new version of the product and will buy more products. They'll tell their friends how much they love the product. They'll post about it on social media, blog about it, and leave great reviews. They'll become the marketing team all companies wish to have: passionate and genuine with unlimited reach. They will become fanatics for your company.

GUIDED REFLECTIONS:

1. What percentage of your customers are fans? How do you know they're fans?

....

2. When's the last time someone in a management or leadership position in your company talked to a fan?

....

3. How are the needs of your customers changing?

....

4. What are you doing as a company to develop products and services to meet the needs of your customers five, ten, or even fifteen years from now?

....

5. Are you able to have honest conversations with your customers about sustainability?

....

6. Would your customers approve of the way you treat your employees?

....

7. Are your customers versed on SDGs and ESG? If they are, then that's even more reason for you to get excited about what we're talking about. If they're not, they will be soon, so it might behoove you to educate them. Better still, create products that get them thinking about SDGs and ESG, exactly like Apple did with its 2019 ads on its advanced privacy measures and customer data protection.

....

8. Are your employees fans? Do they dread coming to work? If your employees aren't enthusiastic or passionate about your company, it will be difficult for your customers to become fans.

....

CHAPTER 10

BRAND IMAGE

"The keys to brand success are self-definition, transparency, authenticity and accountability."

—SIMON MAINWARING

I n September 1982, people in Chicago started dying after taking painkillers. It began when a postal worker woke up with a headache, took an over-the-counter pain reliever, and died suddenly soon after. As more people died, a common link was discovered: each victim had taken Tylenol. An investigation turned up potassium cyanide in the capsules. The pills came from different batches and plants, so the poisonous chemical hadn't been introduced in one batch or in just one plant.

The deadly Tylenol capsules continued turning up at drug stores around Chicago. Eventually, it was discovered that someone was actually tampering with the bottles on the store shelves. This set off a nationwide panic, and poison control hotlines and hospitals were overwhelmed. In Chicago, police went through the streets with loudspeakers warning everyone of the dangers of taking Tylenol.

Johnson & Johnson, the manufacturer of the drug, acted quickly. The company spent millions recalling Tylenol, and stores rushed to remove the product from shelves. Even though the company did the right thing, the tragedy didn't stop immediately, because copycat criminals tainted drugstore pills with hydrochloric acid, rat poison, and other ingredients that sickened people across the country.

And it wasn't just drugs. Other copycats went so far as to tamper with food on grocery shelves, inserting pins and other objects into candy bars. With Halloween approaching, some communities banned trick-or-treating for fear that children would find pins and razors in their candy. I remember this well, because even though I was allowed to trick-or-treat, my mother made my brother and me throw away the apples we'd received in our treat bags. It would be too easy, she believed, for someone to slip something sharp into the fruit.

Leadership at Johnson & Johnson was as transparent as they were proactive in their response and communication. They held public press conferences at the company's headquarters. Tylenol became the first product in the industry to use new tamper resistant packaging, and J&J did it just six months after the crisis. The company created triple-safety-seal packaging that combined a foil seal, a plastic seal, and a sealed box.

The Tylenol scare was tragic for many, but it also had a measurable and positive impact, causing a revolution in product safety standards. Security controls increased in factories, and manufacturing processes were improved. Packaging, in particular, changed dramatically, especially for food and drugs. Tamper-proof seals became the norm, and any consumer could easily tell whether a pill bottle had been opened.

This incident could have destroyed the Johnson & Johnson brand, and the company. But because leadership moved quickly to resolve the issue and prevent further tragedy, they were able to recover and maintain their image. Instead of covering up the problem or pointing fingers, they took on the responsibility, proving that they were still a brand that deserved people's respect. They understood that a company couldn't rest on its laurels but must continuously act in ways to live up to its image.

This kind of action isn't only about protecting a brand, but about crisis management and what that says about a company and its decision makers. It's about disasters that affect a company's customers and what the company's response says about what's important. In this case, Johnson & Johnson put profits aside to focus on the customer's safety, proving that when you resolve a problem ethically, no matter how serious the problem might be, you can survive as a business. And the public will be open to allowing you to regain their trust, instead of shutting you out altogether.

Compare Johnson & Johnson's handling of an incident that could have destroyed their brand, with Mitsubishi Morgan Stanley's handling of the situation detailed in Chapter 5. In that instance, the court case received a lot of media attention in Japan, most of it negative for the company. But what if Mitsubishi Morgan Stanley had taken a more employee-friendly, family-focused path? They could have simply presented an application for paternity leave and then approved the request. How might that plan of action have played out for the company? And how many thousands of people have had similar experiences that have cost the company valuable employees and untold millions?

By promoting paternity leave, the company could have led the industry by example. This would have demonstrated to their investors, employees, and customers that they cared about their people. It might have also gained the attention of the media for another reason: Japan's impending demographic nightmare of a declining workforce. By deterring workers from starting families for fear of losing their jobs, the population of that country continues to decline. Mitsubishi Morgan Stanley had an opportunity to publicize—at no cost to themselves—how they were a shining example of the kind of company people want to invest in, work for, and buy from.

And that's not all. On the back of our efforts of speaking up for parental rights, the Japanese paternity law was recently changed in favor of fathers. (See Figure 5.2.) In June 2021, the House of Representatives passed a bill that granted shorter prior notice for paternity leave (reduced from four weeks to two weeks), guaranteed 80 percent of the father's salary during the paternity leave (increased from 60 percent), and passed a mandate that companies with more than 1,000 employees would have to publish in a public forum how many of their employees are taking child care leave and how many days they're taking (to improve transparency).[72] If Mitsubishi Morgan Stanley had admitted their mistakes and worked towards a better future, they could have taken credit for these changes. It was a branding opportunity par excellence they chose to ignore. The destruction of value and the lost opportunity cost together are immeasurable.

What is a company's image worth? Can you put a price on your brand? That's a difficult question to answer, but we can see how a company's brand benefits them. Consider how much a company has to spend on customer acquisition, or repeat business, or marketing in general. Then look at any business

---

72 "Japan Enacts Law Making Paternity Leave More Flexible for Men," *The Japan Times*, June 3, 2021, https://www.japantimes.co.jp/news/2021/06/03/national/social-issues/japan-law-paternity-leave-flexible-men/.

that has fans who admire the company's brand and consider how much it saves in marketing costs. As Jim Rohn said many years ago, "One customer well taken care of could be more valuable than $10,000 worth of advertising." We would argue that, in today's new world, that $10,000 could easily be millions. Treating employees and customers as brand advocates makes good business sense.

Contrast that with a business that's constantly trying to clean up its image. In an example like Mitsubishi Morgan Stanley, add in the legal costs. Where does your company fall on the brand and image spectrum, from the perspective of your investors, employees, customers, and the world at large?

THE PERCEPTION AND IMPORTANCE OF BRAND IMAGE OVER TIME

In the past, a brand image was concocted by the company it represented. Marketing teams developed an image and branded the company with that image through marketing, advertising, and other communication. That image didn't necessarily reflect the truth about a company or their products, e.g., Philip Morris's Marlboro Man as a representative of masculinity and virility when in fact, tobacco was known to cause deadly diseases such as lung cancer.

Today, companies still try to manipulate their image in the public eye, but people have become sensitive to that type of marketing. They don't trust it. Their "BS meters" have become much more sensitive. People want to know what a business really stands for, and they want to see it in their actions, not in their creative marketing.

The media and global communications networks have accelerated this shift. A brand a few decades ago like Coca-Cola was known by their TV advertising, placement on store shelves, billboards, and by their logo wherever the company could manage to put it. People recognized the logo and the name, but they didn't have a deep relationship with the product or the company. The connection was shallow and static. It didn't change and grow over time.

Today people are bombarded with messaging everywhere, at any time. On a cell phone, a tablet, or a laptop, ads can appear tailored to a person's interests. Through email, social media, and traditional methods like TV and radio advertising, and subway ads and billboards, the message is repeated. We also have the twenty-four-hour news cycle to report any time a company does something that makes them look good or bad.

If a company does something the public doesn't like—such as Pepsi's "tone deaf" television commercial that ran in 2017, which appeared to trivialize the human rights protests of that year—people voice their disapproval about it on Twitter. They call for boycotts. They parody the ad. Late night hosts satirize these egregious marketing missteps. When this happens, the negative impact on a brand can be immediate and disastrous. A similar thing happened with chicken nuggets in McDonald's Japan. Most of those nuggets were made in Thailand, and they discovered pieces of plastic in them. Children had been ingesting the plastic, choking on it—it was awful. Management did the best they could to control the damage, but for years after that, there were jokes and memes that wouldn't go away.

Corporations have a responsibility to build and protect their brand, not by pretending to be something they're not, but by having socially responsible values. Then they have to live up to those values.

Your corporate image is the full definition of who you are in the minds of everyone in society. To the extent that you're operating in a way that adds value to society impacts your balance sheet. It affects consumer decisions as to whether they decide to be your customer. Potential employees and investors want to be associated with a business that has a positive image, not one they're ashamed to put their time and money into. Putting those positive actions into play comes back to the company. It creates a ripple effect and a positivity that, thanks to the internet, social media, globalization, and the Information Age, can reach the far corners of the world.

RISKS AND BENEFITS AROUND A COMPANY'S IMAGE

Companies that don't do the necessary due diligence to manage and communicate their brand image are at risk of making dangerous mistakes that resonate around the world, and thanks to the internet, last forever. Pepsi may have rebounded from their failed attempt at showing consumers what they apparently thought was a timely message, but that awful video will be out there forever.

Companies with damaged brands lose customers. People don't want to support businesses that don't share their values, and they don't only voice their opinions online, they also vote their feelings with their wallets.

Professional partnerships can be strained and perhaps dismantled. Governments and regulatory bodies may be more likely to scrutinize businesses with bad reputations and may make it their mission to expose any wrongdoing.

Investors and shareholders also shy away from companies that have image problems. If you have the choice between putting your money into a company that people love and trust, or into one the public detests, which would you choose? A diminished brand affects the decisions of shareholders, employees, customers, and society. Don't expect anyone's sympathy either. At best, you'll be ignored—at worst, destroyed.

A company that sets high standards for itself and lives up to them has much to gain. It can capitalize on its good behavior by branding itself as a business that benefits society. Everything that a business has to lose with a bad image, it stands to gain with a positive one.

Tokyo Electric and Power Company, TEPCO, learned this lesson the hard way. The Japanese public is well aware of the company's responsibility in the meltdown of March 2011, and their mishandling of the situation in the aftermath. Since the Fukushima disaster, there has been some deregulation in the electric power industry in Japan, including allowing other companies to sell electricity. The competition has tapped into the market share with lower prices bolstered by a lack of trust between TEPCO and its former customers who have consciously chosen to buy their electricity from other sources. TEPCO responded by hiring an army of salespeople, including many third-party contractors, to aggressively contact and try to win back the electric company's customers with deep discounts. However, customers are skeptical. Once a company loses the trust of the public, winning it back is extremely difficult. Brand loyalty cannot simply be bought.

Perhaps one of the most valuable assets a company has to gain with a positive image is the public's trust. People who don't trust a company don't buy from that company unless there's no other option. These companies are ripe for disruption, and their customers are eager to switch brands. For example, in the case of cell phone or internet service, customers can switch providers. People are more discerning and willing to go farther, pay more, or wait in line to patronize a business they trust and respect. In the words of Howard Schultz, the former CEO of Starbucks, "If people believe they share values with a company, they will stay loyal to the brand."

People feel good when they support a reputable business. They are no longer as willing or compliant to suffer feelings of stress or even guilt when forced to purchase from companies they don't respect.

KEY TAKEAWAY

The shift in power around brand image from corporation to customer has put pressure on businesses to act in the best interests of the environment and society. Image isn't just window dressing. It's who a company is, the values that guide them, and the actions that define them. People are watching and there's no longer anywhere to hide.

The best strategy, then, is to align with global guidelines such as Sustainable Development Goals and environmental, social, and governance criteria. Decide who you want to be as a company and stay true to that vision. Authenticity isn't something you can buy or fake. It has to be real, and today's public can tell the difference.

GUIDED REFLECTIONS:

1. What's the brand image of your company, and what can you do to improve it?

....

2. What do you want your brand image to be? Are you moving in that direction?

....

3. How is your company's image and your brand impacting employees in your day-to-day operations? Your relationships with partners, shareholders, the government, and regulatory agencies?

....

4. What are you doing that doesn't align with your desired image, and what can you do differently to correct that misalignment?

....

5. What mistakes have you made around brand image in the past (like Mitsubishi Morgan Stanley)?

....

6. Have you rectified those situations? How?

....

7. Have you learned from those mistakes? What are the key lessons learned?

....

CHAPTER 11

THE NEW CONNECTIVITY

"Everything you do has an impact. Who you are—that you are—actually matters. In an interconnected world (the only kind we have), our actions and the actions of others are inextricably linked—we are always and forever in a dance of mutual influence with those with whom we directly and indirectly participate. It is the unavoidable reality of being social creatures, only magnified by an ever-increasingly complex and interwoven societal structure. We matter to each other."

—Paul Greiner

It's rare for people in Japan to criticize the country. From my perspective, having lived in Canada, the United States, Japan, Mexico, and China, I've gained some perspective on how democratic and capitalist societies operate. At its heart, Japan is still very much the old Japan. It may be dressed up like a progressive country, but it's mostly for show. More than thirty years ago, Karel van Wolferen wrote *The Enigma of Japanese Power*, a seminal work that describes Japanese power structures. It's an astonishing text that lays bare Japan's inner workings, often speaking the unspeakable. I first picked it up after I came back to Japan in 1990, and I've reread it often since then. It's been three decades, and virtually everything in that book is still relevant.

At its core, Japan operates as Japan, Inc. or what van Wolferen calls "the System" or Japanism. This is the industrial economic machine that Japan set up after the Second World War to regenerate its economy from devasting losses. In essence, it's a complete collusion—from citizens all the way up to senior political leaders and the judicial system—to ensure Japanese corporations, and thus the country, win. Japan, Inc. functions less as a political, social, or economic structure, and more as a religion. It requires complete subservience from its citizens, and in return promises peace. Japanese citizens accept this social contract of peace on faith, and through belief in the System's benevolence:

> Although the System may not be Big Brother, the Japanese are asked to accept that it loves them in return for social obedience. This means, among other things, not questioning—at least not continuously and systematically—the political system... In the Western tradition, intellectual probing of the socio-political environment is allowed and sometimes encouraged; the Japanese tradition requires emotional trust.[73]

The contemporary ruling elites in this system have gained their power not through merit, but through the circumstances into which they were born. As we saw with the *amakudari* in Chapter 4, the Japanese System protects "the administrator class by keeping the criteria for membership, and the rules governing

---

73   van Wolferen, *Enigma of Japanese Power*, 202.

transactions among the administrators themselves, informal."[74] This is, according to van Wolferen, the essential criteria for the survival of the Japanese system—that its basis for power and the right to rule is not written in any rulebook, constitution, or law (for then it can be disputed) but is instead based entirely on informal ties.

For years, this system worked well enough to rebuild Japan. Today, however, it is breaking down. Japan has faced thirty years of decline since the bubble burst in the 80s. It has 250 percent debt to the GDP, which is unsustainable. If Japan doesn't change its system soon, it's likely to face thirty more years of decline. Yet, no one is allowed to criticize Japan, Inc. If you have faith in the system and if you offer it your emotional trust, then how can you doubt it, much less criticize it? And if you do doubt or criticize it, then you must be a traitor to the country.

It's a tightrope that Japanese journalists walk all the time—how do you report in a country that "does not reward those who point out its contradictions"?[75] The short answer: they don't. They keep quiet on the scandals and the fraud, and the systematic issues, afraid to report anything that would rend "the fabric of reality as presented by the System."[76] It's the same in Japanese businesses. You don't criticize Japan, Inc. unless you want to get kicked out of the room or criticized to the point that you're no longer able to do business in Japan.

Yet the American athletic shoe company, Nike, put out an ad that did just that. It showcased the experiences of three female soccer players: one who was Japanese, one who was of Korean ethnicity but living in Japan, and one who was of

---

74 van Wolferen, *Enigma of Japanese Power*, 109.

75 van Wolferen, *Enigma of Japanese Power*, 97.

76 van Wolferen, *Enigma of Japanese Power*, 97.

mixed race (her father was black). Nike called it "The Future Isn't Waiting." It showed how these three teenagers overcame bullying over race and other differences to triumph through sport. Certain scenes hit hard. The Korean is shown researching the "Zainichi problem," which is the term for the complex discrimination faced by Koreans in Japan. The girl of mixed race is surrounded by her Japanese classmates as they touch her hair and mock her for its different texture. The ad pushed into the open issues that Japan often buries under that age-old party line of "We're a happy, peaceful nation and there is no discrimination here." The Nike ad said: "There is, and young people are overcoming it."[77]

The video went viral. On YouTube, it began getting a high percentage of likes—60 to 70 percent—with the rest of the audience giving it a thumbs down. Then people came to Japan's defense and the percentages flipped. We don't know if people changed their minds or felt pressured to defend the country out of loyalty, but the video became very controversial. Some people were calling it amazing and powerful; others were calling for a boycott of Nike products. Some government officials commented that the ad didn't honestly depict Japan, and that Nike was just bashing the country for some unknown reason.

However people feel about Japan, the video hit a nerve. It exposed a side of Japanese culture that outsiders never see, a Japan that no one talks about. In a western country the video may have been applauded. It focused on issues that children of any country deal with. But while some cultures are open to conversations about people's struggles, Japan does not like to admit that any of its people, even children, have problems.

---

77   "Nike: The Future Isn't Waiting," Wieden + Kennedy, November 2020, https://www.wk.com/work/
       nike-the-future-isnt-waiting/.

This isn't the first time Japan has eschewed this kind of attention. In 2015, journalist Shiori Itō was raped by one of her bosses. In Japan, sexual abuse, harassment, and rape are frequent occurrences in the workplace. It's just something women, and probably men too, aren't supposed to talk about. Yet, Itō bucked the system by raising her hand and proclaiming that she was raped, and something needed to be done about it. The case went to court and Itō was highly criticized in Japan. As a result, she had to leave the country and is presently living in the UK.

The Nike ad was controversial in Japan, but Itō's case gained attention worldwide. It's a window into the true Japan that nobody likes to talk about: A sexist, often misogynistic and xenophobic society that sees employees, and especially female employees, as property owned by corporations and their leadership, to use as they please, no matter how immoral, unjust, or even illegal. And these cases certainly aren't limited to Japan, but we highlight this as a prime example of attitudes and practices that are unsustainable.

It's also a glimpse into the side of Japan that influences other countries' choices about whether to do business there. Can a country that supports harassment, abuse, and even rape be sustainable in the global marketplace? Does this draconian culture serve the country's society, and how will it affect Japan's future? Boone Pickens, an energy tycoon who made his money through oil and later renewable energy, swore never to do business in Japan for this reason. I heard him speak at a conference where he described his experience, and what he said mirrors what van Wolferen wrote. Japan, Inc. is a rigged system designed to protect the elites, and there's no place for sustainable business practices of the future.

Japan's culture in this respect is obviously out of line with SDG goals. You can't have sustainable development in a country where people don't want to do business. Likewise, GSE criteria (our version of ESG, as corporate governance is the most important of the three factors) calls out social betterment specifically and does not align with employee abuse. A company that has strong and proper corporate governance would not allow this. Can a country with corporations that protect sexual abuse in the workplace, and discourage employees from starting a family, survive?

Japan has had opportunities to change but is yet to embrace them. Take the recent coronavirus pandemic. When COVID-19 hit, governments all over the world shut down restaurants, cinemas, and shops. Most of the global workforce worked from their houses to stop the spread of the disease. Yet in Japan, employees were crowding the subway to get to work because corporations made it mandatory to come to the office. As management saw it, this was how they had always functioned, so this is how they would continue to function. According to Rochelle Kopp, a Japanese business culture expert and cross-cultural communications specialist, the decision was due "partially [to] the paperwork and partially [to] old-fashioned bosses who can't wrap their heads around the idea of remote work."[78] She adds that employees do not have laptops to facilitate work from home.

This was a golden opportunity for Japan to embrace a new way of doing things, while simultaneously protecting its citizens from a deadly disease, and yet it chose the same old, unsustainable way of functioning. This is not the first time Japan has made this choice.

On a macro level, Japan is really run by the *bōryokudan/yakuza* (organized crime/mafia, kanji: 暴力団/ヤクザ), the

---

78   Michael Fitzpatrick, "Why Japan Refuses to Work from Home—Even in a Deadly Pandemic," *Fortune*, June 13, 2021, https://fortune-com.cdn.ampproject.org/c/s/fortune.com/2021/06/13/japan-covid-work-from-home-corporate-culture/amp/.

keidanran (business association, kanji: 経団連), the elite class, and politicians. The *yakuza* plays a surprisingly prominent role, exerting control over crime syndicates and helping the police control non-syndicate crime. In *The Enigma of Japanese Power*, Karel van Wolferen notes that "the *yakuza* are celebrated in the cinema and tolerated in the social landscape."[79] In movies, the *yakuza* are romanticized as symbols of Japanese customs and virtues that have been lost to modernity, such as solidarity with the group and absolute loyalty. "I am obliged to obey the words of my boss at any cost," a member of the *yakuza* said in a police interview, "If he said that a crow is white, I would say it is white. If I had to wear white clothes [be killed in gang warfare] or wear blue clothes [go to prison] as a result of that, I would accept it."[80]

The *yakuza* and the other elite organizations don't seem to realize that unsustainable business practices—allowing harassment of employees, allowing rape of women, firing women for getting pregnant—are more damaging than helpful to not only society, but to the country and its future in global business. These practices are directly contradictory to what Japan's corporations are saying about themselves in terms of SDGs, ESG, and sustainability in general. If these practices were reversed and a more sustainable path was followed, the upside would be unlimited. Sustaining the business practices that we recommend in this book would solve most of the "biggest problems" of modern Japan—and perhaps a lot of countries.

In Japan, *honne* refers to the authentic self. It's the truth about who a person is, and when applied to business, how a company truly operates. The opposite of *honne* is *tatemae*—public brand or persona—which refers to people, and by

---

79 van Wolferen, *Enigma of Japanese Power*, 101.

80 van Wolferen, *Enigma of Japanese Power*, 101.

extension, companies. *Tatemae* is what you show to others, what you want others to perceive you as. If there's any dirty laundry, you make sure you hide it. I call it the Mickey Mouse Syndrome. Have you ever seen how Disneyland is run behind the scenes? No? That's because they have a whole underground system to keep those operations hidden from you. When you walk around Disneyland, all you see is the perfect sets, the green grass and blue skies, the smiling characters. Meanwhile, in secret lanes, someone is ferrying away the garbage, making sure there is enough food in the restaurants and that the shows start on time. Even the lofty towers are an optical illusion, designed with progressively shorter layers that narrow as they rise, giving the false appearance of height and distance. That's kind of like what *tatemae* is—it's pretending everything is perfect, as if no one is working behind the scenes.

When someone's *tatemae* isn't aligned with their *honne*, it's merely a façade intended to save face, or *mentsu*. Rather than actually becoming the person or company they want the world to see, companies whose *honne* and *tatemae* are in sharp contrast choose to protect their supposed honor by projecting this false image of themselves.

This is precisely how Japan, Inc. functions as well. The elite organizations have built an extraordinarily thick wall between their *honne*—the reality of how Japan functions—and their *tatemae*—what they project to the world. Then they bought control of the media so that no stories can be published that contradict this vision. That's why you don't hear stories of Boone Pickens in the media. It's why Shiori Itō daring to speak out was so important. Her voice attacked that thick wall Japan, Inc. has built around who they really are; she cracked it. We need more stories like hers, and like mine, that help crack the armor of *tatemae*, so that Japan changes. If it does not, then this country that I cherish is likely to face perpetual decline, probably beyond the point of repair within the next couple of decades.

Of course, we've seen a similar wall between *honne* and *tatemae* before—with the Great Financial Crisis. Exactly like Japan, Inc., the fraudulent corporations and the rating companies in the United States created an internal system that had its own elite club of people who knew the truth and vowed to stay quiet because their pockets were being lined. On the outside, for *tatamae*, they marketed their impartiality, their infallibility, and their honesty—all of it lies. They were able to keep the con going for a while, but in the end, the wall always crumbles and the truth, *honne*, is exposed.

Companies that operate with misaligned *honne* and *tatemae* are known to others in the business world, but the subject is never broached. It's business's dirty little secret, and until a few years ago, that secret was safe from public knowledge. People believed, to a certain extent, that a company stood for whatever it purported to stand for. They believed whatever branding the marketing people put out there for public consumption.

A WORLD CONNECTED OVER TIME

Several generations ago, if you wanted to know what it was like to work at a company, you had to ask someone who worked there, and then hope they told you the truth. If it was a large company, the information wasn't reliable because of the many departments and chains of command. That person might work in a different division than the one you were applying to work in, so anything they told you about the business reflected their limited perspective.

A couple of decades ago when I was completing my MBA at Wharton, I networked with people directly to find out what it was like to work at Merrill Lynch, which is where I began my financial career. I met with about fifty people from the company. Books had been published about what it was like behind the scenes at some companies, but still, the visibility into how businesses operated was nonexistent compared to the access we have today. The change has been revolutionary. Today, I can go online and find hundreds of people at a corporation to talk to me about what their company is really like.

The internet and social media have leveled the playing field, giving everyone an equal voice on the world stage. Sites like Glassdoor are platforms where employees can safely tell the whole truth about what it's like to work at a certain company, including salary, culture, and management (or mismanagement) details. In essence, this new world has allowed anyone at any company to air that company's dirty laundry, expose its true self, and show the world the distinct and sometimes alarming disparities that exist between who a company really is and the public brand or persona it pretends to be. Likewise, the great things about a company can also be highlighted and discussed.

GLASSDOOR: A BEHIND-THE-SCENES GLIMPSE INTO THE WORKPLACE

Sites such as *Glassdoor.com*, where employees post candid workplace reviews anonymously, provide a telling glimpse into what it's really like to work at some of the biggest companies in the world.

"...the worst company I have ever worked at...stay away!"
—ANONYMOUS QUOTE FROM A FORMER MITSUBISHI EMPLOYEE

Nobody's perfect, and no company is perfect. We all have dirty laundry, and we'd like it to remain hidden. But when that laundry negatively affects the rights of a company's employees, or impacts its customers, its investors, or even the environment, covering it up isn't acceptable. This is no longer just an ethical issue, because thanks to the new connectivity, that dirty laundry will be exposed, and the negative impact won't only be on employees and investors—it can bring down the company itself.

Shiori Itō connected with the world through the internet to tell the world her story. She shared how she had been raped and was told by her employer to keep quiet. The legal case, where lawyers argued that the rape never happened, exposed the ridiculous nature of Japan's court system.

For example, one of the arguments the company used, was that rape couldn't have occurred because the windows in the perpetrator's office were open that day. The court embraced this type of argument because their goal isn't justice, but to squash the credibility of any person who puts up their hand. From an article in *Japan Times,* a former judge said, "The Japanese judiciary is extremely sheltered and full of bureaucratic elites. In such a world, the principle of strict hierarchy reigns supreme, while any individuals who are liberal-minded and outspoken are purged."[81]

They'll embrace any story that supports that goal, rather than seek justice and the truth. The goal is merely to hang onto the old way of doing business. Companies and the courts want employees to follow the traditional, standard operating procedures. As van Wolferen says, "...nothing in their history encourages ordinary Japanese citizens to think that the law

---

81 Tomohiro Osaki, "Ex-Judge Lifts Lid on Japan's 'Corrupt' Judicial System," *The Japan Times,* April 30, 2014, https://www.japantimes.co.jp/tag/hiroshi-segi/.

exists to protect them. Never adding up to a system based on rational, philosophical principles of justice, traditional Japanese law consisted of little more than lists of commands to be blindly obeyed by commoners."[82]

Nowhere has this corruption at the heart of the judicial system been more exposed as in *Courts without Hope* (*Zetsubo no Saibansho*), written by Hiroshi Segi, an ex-Supreme Court Judge. Segi was so disillusioned with the judiciary that he left it to become a professor, at which point he wrote his memoir describing bone-chilling incidents where top judges talk openly about purging junior judges from their positions based on their leftist ideologies.[83] One judge, Hironobu Takesaki, punished any junior judge who published papers counter to Takesaki's leadership by denying them promotion and banishing them to the rural areas of Japan. The result? No one dared go against him. It's exactly what we saw in Chapter 6, in Enron and other corrupt corporations—anyone who doesn't follow the party line is punished and made to leave. This is how you establish a system that always rules in favor of the elites and the status quo.

In other words, young men and women should know that when they join a large corporation in Japan, they are giving up many human rights. They are sacrificing their dreams to the system. They are married first to the company, and maybe second to a partner. If the boss asks a female employee to stay behind after a drinking party and sleep with him, that's what the woman is supposed to do. They are expected to do it with a smile on their face and go into work the next day as if nothing had happened. It's part of the job, and they must "enjoy" it as a "benefit" of the job which they are "privileged" to have. While

82   van Wolferen, *Enigma of Japanese Power*, 209.

83   Hiroshi Segi, *Zetsubo no Saibansho* (Tokyo, Japan: Kodansha Ltd., 2014).

instances like this may not be as prevalent as in the past, this is still by and large the expectation. Anyone who dares speak out against it is deemed an enemy of the country. The courts won't protect them.

On the contrary, we speak up here because we cherish Japan and our Japanese families, and we want to see Japan and her corporations be wildly successful. In no way is this book meant to be a critique of Japan, by the way. This is about sustainable business practices, and these issues can be found anywhere, in any country. I just happen to be very well-versed with Japan because it's a country that I know and deeply revere—and a country where I've lived and worked for a very long time.

All of this has its roots in Japan, Inc. As we mentioned, Japan, Inc. functions on faith and the belief in the benevolence of the ruling elite. Japanese citizens trust that the System will take care of them because it's meant to be good and virtuous. But this rhetoric allows no space for human rights. If you're asked to believe—indeed, trust blindly—that a system is benevolent and that everyone has your best interests at heart, then there's no need for you to have human rights. And if you're asking for human rights, then it's clear that your belief in the System is not strong enough. You're not loyal to the country. Thus:

> Individuals are not believed to exist for and of themselves as autonomous entities; only the state does. In Japan, state sovereignty is heaven-granted while individual rights are bestowed by the state. The state allows limited individual rights to the extent that they further the aims of the state. Thus, individual rights are always instruments of the state, not to be utilised for the aims of the individual.[84]

---

84   van Wolferen, *Enigma of Japanese Power*, 209.

It's this rhetoric that allows Japan to dismiss human rights issues and thus dismiss sustainability, even when they directly clash with treaties they've signed as members of the United Nations (*tatemae*). Carlos Ghosn's story is a good example. So is that of Vincent Fichot.

Fichot is a victim of the very rigid gender roles in Japanese society. In Japan, women are seen as guardians of the home and family, and men are meant to work. This creates a lopsided power dynamic in child custody battles—courts almost always rule in favor of the woman when it comes to child custody and they do not allow joint custody in Japan. Some women misuse this, essentially using the child as a sword over their partner's head. If the partner doesn't do what they want, the woman will up and leave with the child and the man will have no recourse to get his son or daughter back, or to even see his children ever again.

This is what happened to Frenchman Vincent Fichot. Despite trying everything through the Japanese legal system, the European Union, and even the French Prime Minister, Fichot hasn't been able to see his kids. During the Olympics of 2021, he took the last option open to him: he went on a hunger strike outside the stadium to draw attention to his case. These custody issues are so rampant, there's even an organization created called Find My Parent. Bear in mind that Japan has signed the Hague Convention that allows joint custody—yet in reality, they don't implement it. It's *honne* and *tatemae* all over again.

This duplicity can be seen in countries all over the world, not just in Japan. But it isn't necessary. Japan can be wildly successful, but it can only do that if it embraces change and adopts the sustainable practices we talk about in this book. Karel van Wolferen wrote *The Enigma of Japanese Power* thirty years ago, and it's relevant today. Passages from Segi's *Courts*

Without Hope could have been from the same book, and yet they were written decades apart. What does that say about how committed Japan is to change? Sharing these stories and talking about them openly puts pressure on Japan to reform. And in reforming, it may ensure its own survival. This is what I, and those who have an attachment to this country, hope for.

Today's new connectivity is flushing out these bad actors, though not as quickly as some would like. Modern companies understand that hiding the truth is not the best option, and that even if they've behaved badly in the past, coming clean about their misdeeds and trying to do better is the best course of action. Everyone loves a person who's trying to improve themselves, and everyone loves a company that's trying to do better.

RISKS AND BENEFITS AROUND CONNECTIVITY

Shiori Itō's company missed out on an opportunity to admit their wrongdoing and pledge to be a better company for their employees. They could have supported her and used the case as a springboard to announce a change in policies that would protect victims of harassment in their offices. They could have gained worldwide attention for that change in policy and stood out as a role model for other Japanese corporations and how business is done today in Japan. The world would have embraced that message, and given them extensive coverage— free marketing, basically. The television time and newspaper coverage would have made the company famous worldwide, in a positive way, and potentially saved them millions in legal fees fighting the case and in marketing trying to do damage control (much like the Morgan Stanley Mitsubishi video we discussed in Chapter 5).

People are looking for *real*, they're looking for *sincere*—

not just these disingenuous corporations that are too big to care. Corporations that feel they're too big to care might find themselves facing irrelevance. People would want to work for a company that stands up for its employees, instead of worrying that accepting a job is an invitation to harassment and abuse. Hiring costs would likely be down and retention rates, up. Productivity in the company can skyrocket with all the positive publicity. Companies that avoided working with them in the past might reach out, seeing that they are turning over a new leaf. Once you admit that you've made a mistake, show remorse, and make the effort to change, people can be unbelievably forgiving and supportive. But first you have to be honest about the mistake.

In my own court case, it finally came out that all the evidence supporting my defense had been destroyed. There were pages and pages of emails, schedules, and other documentation that weren't allowed to be viewed initially, because Mitsubishi Morgan Stanley claimed it contained sensitive information. Those documents included just basic things like schedules, meeting notes, meeting room numbers, records. When the time came to finally show it to the judge, lawyers claimed it no longer existed. Mitsubishi Morgan Stanley had destroyed the key evidence in a court case against them.

As of the time of this writing, the courts have failed to take action against Mitsubishi Morgan Stanley, even though it was obvious what they had done. Japanese courts are often in a hurry to process civil cases because their speed "is considered a vital barometer of their competence."[85] In that context, any case where the parties don't settle out of court is considered troublesome. According to Segi, judges try and convince plain-

---

85   Segi, *Zetsubo no Saibansho*.

tiffs to drop cases so that it can be considered "completed" and they can move to the next one. Van Wolferen echoes a similar sentiment: "...[judges] are not inclined to take time absorbing the arguments of plaintiffs who may already have irritated them by rejecting their advice for a settlement out of court." Moreover, they tend to be unsympathetic to any life experience that falls out of their own purview. For example, "...in cases involving industrial accidents, they [judges] have been known to imply that plaintiffs knew the risks they were taking in deciding to work in a dangerous place."[86] In a poll taken in 2007, only 24 percent of plaintiffs were happy with how their cases were handled.[87]

I've faced similar bias in my own case. I remember this like it was yesterday. We were all in the judge's chambers. My lawyer and I were sitting on one side, Mitsubishi Morgan Stanley's representatives and their lawyers were on the other side. The judge was opposite us, studying the list of witnesses we'd submitted for the trial. My lawyers had given the names of eight witnesses that would testify against the company, and Mitsubishi Morgan Stanley had submitted a similar list of eight or nine names.

The judge, Mr. Kenkichi Sakuma, looked up and said—in his infinite wisdom—that he had decided to allow all of Mitsubishi Morgan Stanley's witnesses to testify and none of mine. My lawyer stepped in immediately and asked if that was a fair decision. The judge told my lawyers he'd made up his mind, at which point I couldn't stay quiet. As politely as possible and in Japanese, I asked him to reconsider. "If you're hoping to reach the truth of a dispute, how can you only hear one side of the story?" I asked.

---

86   van Wolferen, *Enigma of Japanese Power*, 220.

87   Segi, *Zetsubo no Saibansho*.

What happened next is almost exactly as Segi and van Wolferen described it. The judge wouldn't look at me. Instead, he looked at my lawyers and, clearly furious, he began berating them. It was their job as my Japanese advocates to keep me, this foreigner, under control. It was clear to him I didn't understand the Japanese system at all, because otherwise I wouldn't even have spoken to him.

Some have suggested that the judges/courts were bribed in my case. Although I would never want to suggest that, it certainly would explain many of the very bizarre events in this case as well as many of the actions by the courts. It would also support the core role of the "system" as outlined by Segi and Von Wolferen amongst others. That is, to protect Japan Incorporated and to protect the behemoth "Too Big to Care" corporations like Mitsubishi. A bribe, by these standards, would be considered an act of honor to protect the mighty "system."

This is how entrenched bias and tradition are in the Japanese judiciary—judges are so encased in a particular system, they cannot even recognize the need for change, forget campaign for it. Nor is there any hope of progress unless the system itself changes. Currently, judges are picked right out of law school and indoctrinated into this way of thinking. As we mentioned, anyone who doesn't follow the pre-set path is purged from the ranks. Segi believes there's a greater chance for justice if judges are picked out of a group of experienced lawyers instead: "Truly good lawyers are more likely to be concerned about the feelings of litigants, and able to respect their human rights."[88]

Till then, however, litigants must use the world's new connectivity to fight for justice. I left those chambers and created the first YouTube video about what I had faced at Mitsubishi

---

88 Segi, *Zetsubo no Saibansho*.

Morgan Stanley and what had happened in that room. I asked people to come out in support to protest outside the courtroom on the appointed date. The video went viral. The court was flooded with phone calls by outraged citizens. People wanted to know when the court date was, they were asking for directions to court. The video now has 2 million views.

In the end, the protest never happened because the court canceled the date and rescheduled it to eliminate the risk of the crowd. But thanks to all that pressure, the judge allowed one of my witnesses to testify.

The new connectivity between people in different countries and between people and the media has forced some companies to adopt greater transparency. But again, those that are protected by the courts and governments, like Mitsubishi Morgan Stanley, are still enjoying a temporary reprieve. Until their bad deeds catch the attention of the public, they're free to operate with little concern for what their investors, employees, and customers think about them.

In the meantime, companies will continue to be exposed. When I was being harassed by Mitsubishi Morgan Stanley and it looked like I would talk, the company sent me a letter warning me that speaking to the press would result in them "taking necessary action." In other words, they realized the threat posed by the media. Their letter didn't work, of course, and I spoke up. It's easier now for millions of employees around the world to do the same. Anyone can buy a domain and set up a website where they can blog—anonymously if they like—about what goes on behind the scenes in the workplace. People can go on social media sites and call out companies and individuals by name, reaching millions on platforms like Twitter or Facebook. Reviews on Google and Glassdoor allow anyone to provide feedback about businesses to anyone with internet access.

Online petitions are a very visible and direct way of leveraging the new connectivity for the betterment of society. They are a way for anyone who believes in a cause and wants to make that cause public to garner public support. They provide exposure to the whole world, and also allow individuals to raise money for their cause. Parental rights advocates set up and established a petition around my own cause on the website Change.org. The petition, "Zero-Tolerance for Workplace Harassment in Japan," has gained over 30,000 signatures so far, at virtually zero cost, and we expect it to continue to grow.[89] They also set up a homepage at www.patahara.com. Petitions, homepages and blogs that get enough attention can effect a change in laws, in public policy, and in how a company does business.

The anonymity of the internet allows people to speak freely without worrying about repercussions for saying anything negative about their employer. Of course, this also allows people to be less than truthful in their responses, but I believe the truth outweighs the falsehoods when it comes to anonymous company reviews. They reveal things that companies might prefer to remain hidden, but they also force business leaders' hands to adopt a different strategy that's more sustainable. It's making companies look at who they are and what they want to be, and many are moving toward a culture that they can proudly show to the world.

People are also open to discussing their employers without anonymity through professional networking sites like LinkedIn. I've personally been contacted by individuals looking for information about what it's like to work for different financial

89   The petition is available in seven languages. You can find the English version here: http://chng.it/vgcpt8Lzjc. The Japanese version can be found here: https://www.change.org/p/mufg-morgan-stanley-zero-tolerance-for-workplace-harassment-in-japan.

institutions in Japan, and I've given people honest responses, both the positive and the negative. This is invaluable information for a person with a critically important decision to make that could impact their life for years to come. I care about that person making a good decision, so I'm very honest about my experiences. Many corporations, both Japanese and multinational, have contacted me seeking consulting services on how to promote more sustainable workplaces and avoid PR disasters such as those that Mitsubishi Morgan Stanley created.

When you consider the power of circles, and how each action has a reaction in the world, and how all those reactions have a way of coming back to you, you can see how helping other people isn't only good for them, it's good for you too. That person knows they can trust me, and so I become a more trustworthy person. I tell them which companies are still stuck in the past and will make their life miserable, and which ones have a global culture with best management practices driven out of world business centers like New York or London.

I feel good sending bright, talented college graduates to the best companies. Those firms deserve the best, and the best deserve to work there. They will both be better and stronger due to those relationships, and they will handily outlive firms that don't truly value their people. Those companies will have reputations that stand up to scrutiny, because they are who they say they are.

I believe that if you throw a stone into the pond of the universe, the ripples continue forever. Helping someone make the right career move can pay off in many ways you may never see, but I believe that telling the truth has positive ripples. On the other hand, lying makes for negative ripples that extend out as well. Negative karma will return to the sender.

In the power of circles, what goes around comes around. A

business that makes the news for nefarious activities will feel the impact of their actions for years to come through social networks that reach their investors, their employees, and their customers. Some highly motivated groups or individuals may even publish a book and become lifelong advocates for the cause.

Those who refuse to change and adapt to the visibility offered by global connectivity will eventually become irrelevant. In some cases, the transformation will take longer due to factors discussed in the previous chapter. A business that's tied closely to the government and has direct access to political influence, taxpayer money, and the media may be able to carry on for a while. Businesses participating in state-sponsored corruption delay progress, but the end is inevitable. They are not operating in a vacuum, and the world will catch up to them. People will catch on to them.

Transparency is gaining momentum. Companies that fall behind will fall at an ever-accelerating rate. The obvious solution is to act sooner rather than later. Japan's sudden latching on to the concept of SDGs appears as a last-ditch effort to get on board and show the world they're not as bad as they seem. Some are sincerely ready to get on board. The problem is that despite these efforts, the political and business backbone of the country is still stuck in a rut of feudalistic harassment-based management. And so the struggle continues.

Honne—being one's authentic self—is winning out at some Japanese companies. But *tatemae*—brand façade—is still the overriding culture among many large organizations. The trend these days is to wear an SDG lapel pin. It's a badge that shows you and your company support Sustainable Development Goals. Yet, for most, it's merely posturing, like splashing a little paint on the old barn or putting lipstick on the proverbial pig.

It's no better than an expensive colorful brochure with photos of rainforests and mothers cradling their children. The whole while, these companies are still committing destructive acts to families and the environment. They wear the badge at work and later on at parties where they take advantage of employees, as if it allows a person the right to trample on others.

KEY TAKEAWAY

Saying that you have high standards and lofty goals is one thing but taking action to manifest them is another. Companies that want to improve their brand image can start by looking at who they're pretending to be. What is it about that image that's so attractive to investors, employees, customers, and the media? Why not start there and try to live up to that image.

Look at the brochures stacked up in your waiting room. Read your own press releases and marketing collateral—is it truthful and transparent, or is it propaganda that's no longer worth the time and effort? Examine the image you are spending so much money to portray and figure out how much of a stretch it would be to actually align your business with that image.

GUIDED REFLECTIONS:

1. Has your company embraced this new connectivity? Do you know what it is and where your business fits?

....

2. Do you have a digital presence? Are you participating in it?

....

3. What is your reputation on Glassdoor?

....

4. What are people saying about your company on Twitter?

....

5. Are there any online petitions that mention your company?

....

6. If you Google your business and yourself, what do you see?

....

7. Are your honne and tatemae aligned, or far apart? What about your online image versus reality?

....

8. How does what others say about your company compare with what your company says about itself?

....

9. Calculate the costs both real and perceived and do a past, present, and future cost analysis. Make brave assumptions where necessary and (if you are not senior management or a senior political leader) try to communicate your findings to management/top leaders.

....

CHAPTER 12

LEADERSHIP AND MANAGEMENT BEST PRACTICES

"Management is doing things right; leadership is doing the right things."

—PETER DRUCKER

A bigail Johnson is the daughter of Ned Johnson, who is the founder of Fidelity. After taking on the role of CEO, she noted that Fidelity had a harassment problem. Two portfolio managers were let go, and Johnson addressed the company's 40,000 employees via video, stating that harassment would not be tolerated. She then formed a sexual harassment response committee at Fidelity, a team that included people from human resources, the company's business side, and an outside lawyer. Fidelity now mandates sexual harassment training.

Consultants always tell leaders to get involved after sexual harassment allegations, but most do the bare minimum. As Jena McGregor writes for the *Washington Post*: "For many CEOs, that means filming a video to share with employees, sending an email reminder about the company's policies, or attending anti-harassment training programs. But Fidelity Investments CEO Abigail Johnson is taking that to the next level—literally."[90] Johnson—CEO of the largest investment company in the US and the world's richest person in finance—moved her office from the seventh floor to the eleventh floor so she could personally monitor the issue and manage it herself.

This was a fantastic way of dealing with the situation. There are those who would argue that she only shifted offices because her consultants told her to, or perhaps because it would look good to the press. Others would say it's simply a reflection of her value system that she reacted so strongly. I would argue that it doesn't matter. What matters is that she took a genuinely powerful, action-oriented stand when the world was watching, and in doing so, she set the stage for how seriously Fidelity considered the issue. Perhaps she had personal experiences that drove her to take massive action, but whatever inspired her to act, she made it clear: Fidelity was not trying to run away from the problem, bury it, delegate it to some line manager with little to no power, or erase it by spinning a positive story about women in leadership positions that they then print in their many fancy brochures. They were not playing games. Under her leadership, they were going to admit to the problem, and then implement steps to fix it.

Abigail teaches us that sustainable leadership and management starts at the top. Fixing problems at your company starts with you, especially if you're in senior management or an executive. Don't expect someone at a lower level in the business to

---

90 Jena McGregor, "After Sexual Harassment Cases, Fidelity's CEO Has Moved Her Office Close to Fund Managers," *The Washington Post*, November 22, 2017, https://www.washingtonpost.com/news/on-leadership/wp/2017/11/22/ after-sexual-harassment-cases-fidelitys-ceo-has-moved-her-office-close-to-fund-managers/.

start a movement that catches on and moves up the ranks. It shouldn't have to work that way. Leaders are the role models that set the standard for how everyone else behaves. If Abigail Johnson hadn't led the response to those harassment claims, do you think anything would have been done? It's up to leaders to captain their ship and lead by example, like Abigail did. If more CEOs responded in the same way, we would have more sustainability in our organizations overall, and of course less harassment.

Compare Abigail's approach with how Mitsubishi Morgan Stanley handled their claims of harassment. The CEO of Mitsubishi Morgan Stanley made a statement in the media that the company had a rampant harassment problem, but that he was going to get rid of all the harassment in the company. Then he disappeared. If the destruction of evidence in the court case is any indication, the answer is clear. His statement was just more *tatemae*—smoke and mirrors meant to distract from the grave reality. What were the specific measures? Did they work? Do employees feel safer and taken care of? We don't know because we didn't hear any more about it. We didn't see any results. It was all smoke and mirrors—deception.

The effects of these two leadership styles are very clear. Companies like Fidelity and Tylenol accepted that their missteps were in the public domain, so they leveraged it to talk to the media and explain what they were doing about the problem. They didn't offer some token apology and empty promises. They took massive actions, and those actions led to an enormous amount of good press. Mitsubishi Morgan Stanley, on the other hand, has spent millions of dollars on my case alone trying to do damage control for all the negative press they've generated, but they won't fix the problem. Which of these two approaches do you think is more circular? Which one creates sustainable businesses?

The following table provides a quick summary of what works and what doesn't:

SUSTAINABLE LEADERSHIP PRACTICES	UNSUSTAINABLE LEADERSHIP PRACTICES
Example: Fidelity, Johnson and Johnson	Example: Mitsubishi Morgan Stanley, Toshiba, Enron
Action-oriented	Lots of talk and no action; PR spend
Rapid in response Focus on truth and facts	Smoke and mirrors approach, with lots of token gestures rather than a real response. Slow to move. Deceptive.
Results in positive press, and a brand image boost rather than a decline Resources dedicated to solution	Results in negative press, and millions of dollars being spent in damage control Resources dedicated to cover-up, lies, putting out fires, legal problems, propaganda
Hands-on top management, and so the whole organization follows their lead to take harassment and complaints very seriously Follow-up until resolved; dedication	Top management that talks but doesn't really address the problem Then silence; sweep under the carpet; nothing to see here strategy...
Perpetrators were fired, in the case of Fidelity. Johnson and Johnson recalled all their products and involved law enforcement to find the perpetrators.	Prayers and promises, rather than actually rooting out the perpetrators and dealing with them. At the end of the day, the perpetrators remain in the organization. Protected as loyal "soldiers."
CONCLUSION: PROGRESS, GROWTH, RESOLUTION ALL STAKEHOLDERS BENEFIT AND VALUE IS CREATED	CONCLUSION: DECLINE, NEGATIVE SPIRAL, CAN KICKED DOWN THE ROAD, PROBLEM GROWS, SOLUTION BECOMES MORE ELUSIVE ALL STAKEHOLDERS SUFFER AND VALUE IS DESTROYED

It's abundantly clear which leadership approach and management practice makes more sense. It's also simple math: if you choose a sustainable path of leadership, then you're ensuring your company survives, thrives, and you're going to set the standard by which everyone is remembered. It's a win-win. Yet senior leaders are hesitant to act on it because they view it as risky. They see it as sticking their neck out. But this is the wrong way to approach it—if you approach it with that mentality, you're going to end up like Enron.

In fact, it is riskier today to not act in a sustainable manner and to ignore these problems, especially with the conversation around ESG strategies and SDGs. If you choose the unsustainable path of leadership, then you're essentially saying you don't mind your company going out of business. As a leader, do you want to be responsible for that?

In the past, and even in some businesses today, leaders tended to overlook personnel problems. They left them to HR, and HR didn't want to get rid of a top producer. That might annoy senior management and put their own job at risk. This is why the responsibility goes beyond human resources and falls squarely on the shoulders of those at the top, people like Abigail Johnson.

In fact, leaders should institute third-party audits. Companies audit their finances, so why should HR be ignored? If you care about corporate governance and your company's social policies, then you should have multiple layers of third parties who are evaluating your management structure, handling your whistleblower protection programs, and finding out what your employees think. If you don't have these third-party systems in place—because internal systems don't cut it—then you'll end up having to handle your dirty laundry in public.

In this era, there's less and less room for yes-men managers, for people who think they're too big to care, for those who aren't thinking about the social, environmental, and corporate governance impact of their actions. If you have a culture that promotes any of these in your senior leadership, you're going to find it quickly becomes unsustainable. So choose carefully.

BAD MANAGERS VS. GOOD LEADERS

Have you heard the old golf analogy about leadership best practices? A good golfer is skilled at knowing when to use which golf club. If he is ten meters from the hole, he uses a putter. If he is twenty-five meters from the hole, he may choose a chipper and, at one hundred meters, a driver may be best. In short, there is no one golf club that is the best to use in every situation.

It is the same with leadership and management best practices. There is no one best management strategy, and a good leader picks from a range of them depending on the context.

Today, there is a lack of leadership and management training. Most of the managers don't have business degrees, and they have never had a management class or course. If the company does offer training, then it is usually in the form of a retreat and a drinking party. People are made leaders not because they possess the correct skillset, or even the aptitude to develop that skillset, but because they have hung around in the company for long enough.

This creates all sorts of problems. These new "leaders" are often bullies because their managers were bullies, and they promote what they know and love. Their employees' problems are ignored in favor of keeping harmony in this elite group. Action is rarely taken against a manager, and if an employee has a complaint, it is rarely ever addressed. As long as this group can go out drinking after work or play basketball together, they are happy. If

one of them wants to fire a pregnant woman, the rest won't inter-
fere. As far as they are concerned, it is the manager's prerogative.

This creates a cycle of bad management. Not only do the
bullies support, protect, and always agree with each other, but
they also hire more bullies to fill positions of power. They're
afraid to promote anyone else because it will show how bad
they are at their jobs. They are invested in holding onto their
power for as long as they can. They try to "lead by fear" and
are afraid to give up control.

BAD MANAGERS	GOOD LEADERS
Leads by fear	Leads by example
Assumes they are better or higher than their workforce, and seeks to command them	Operates on the basis of servant leadership—works with their workforce to create change
Hires and promotes people who are worse than they are, and won't make them look bad	Hires and trains people who they believe will be better than they are
Aims to keep everything as is, and stay in power for as long as possible	Aims to make the company a better place than when they were there
Focus on self	Focus on value generation
Does things "right"—follows the laid-out path and never rocks the boat, no matter how illegal or wrong the current path is	Does the right things—follow their conscience, and works according to principles to create positive change
DETRACTS VALUE	**ADDS VALUE**
NEGATIVE CYCLE OF VALUE DESTRUCTION	**GROWTH, PROGRESS, VALUE INCREASES**

The only way to break this cycle is through training and
practice. It's not impossible for managers to become good
leaders, but they must be willing to learn and implement what

they've learned, no matter how much effort it takes. As Wharton professor Michael Useem says, "There's no medication to make you a leader, no pill you can take, no simple solution for it."[91]

Today's savvy manager recognizes the new connectivity in the world and realizes that any issues impacting the overall company culture, productivity, and sustainability have to be dealt with clearly and decisively. If there's a problem, they admit it; then they take specific actions that demonstrate they are accepting responsibility and are addressing the problem head on.

This might mean firing some of your most influential people if they're participating in this behavior. But this is where change begins, because it demonstrates that you value people who foster values that make for long-term sustainability over people who prioritize short-term profitability at the expense of the company's values.

Sustainability isn't possible in a culture that tolerates powerful employees abusing and harassing other employees. It is management's responsibility to support the business by ridding it of bad actors that bring the whole staff down with their behavior, no matter how smart, talented, or productive they are. When a manager has the courage to take a stand against the most powerful people causing the most damage, they have earned the right to pin an SDG badge on their lapel.

The new connectivity has made it more difficult for companies to tolerate bad behavior in their ranks. Both men and women are more inclined to speak out, knowing they'll find

91   Knowledge at Wharton Staff, "Learning to Be a Better Leader," *Knowledge at Wharton*, July 20, 2021, https://knowledge.wharton.upenn.edu/article/learning-to-be-a-better-leader/?utm_source=kw_newsletter&utm_medium=email&utm_campaign=2021-07-20.

support online, and less inclined to keep quiet about how they're mistreated. Children of the employees may also talk, as they are victims when their parents are being harassed. And it's not the harasser who takes the brunt of the blame—it's the leadership that knowingly allowed it to happen in the first place and continue unchecked. They are as guilty as the perpetrator, or guiltier because they may be ignoring multiple crimes and negatively affecting more lives than just one perpetrator.

As a leader, if you think you can avoid liability by ignoring the problem, you are wrong. No longer can management simply say, "Oh, he's just being a guy. Really, he's a nice person. He has a wonderful family, and he makes us good money. Maybe you just need to let it slide." If a lawsuit was brought against a company, they'd often just settle with the plaintiff. Bad management is costing your company dearly.

TODAY'S LEADER AS CORPORATE CITIZEN

The CEO or anyone leading a public corporation is responsible for the goal of assuring profitability while adding extraordinary value to society. To accomplish that goal, they must play to their strengths and exude honesty, integrity, and a willingness to accept who they are as an individual and who their company is and find ways to move toward sustainability. They have to realize their own and the company's pitfalls, admit their mistakes, and commit to creating a better culture for their people. They should commit to some higher standard, such as SDG and ESG goals. They should also let it be known that they wish for their partners, employees, and customers to move in the same direction.

Equally, and especially in this new connected world, they must be sensitive to the cultural nuances of the markets they're operating in. I did a master's thesis on cultural due diligence and the costs of doing business, and you will be amazed at how many companies ignore this essential foundation. Managers today are often narrow-minded in their approach; they assume everyone they interact with has the same sensibilities as them.

Mindsets and working styles, however, differ dramatically across the globe. "When in Rome, do as the Romans do" does not apply to illegal, non-sustainable, nefarious, misogynistic, or discriminatory actions! That is why the UN is establishing global and universal sustainability goals. When you're working with people from different countries and cultures, you need to take the time to understand where they're coming from, within legal/regulatory limits of course.

This applies to almost every business today. Whether you have multiple offices around the world or are situated locally but are speaking to clients and suppliers from different countries, or are looking to expand into new territories, cultural due diligence is a must. Typically, a company looking to expand will do due diligence on how much it costs to hire people in a new country, buy furniture, acquire new customers, and rent out office space. But they never ask: What percentage of our hires are going to be local hires? What percentage are not going to speak English? How many of our new employees have a different background from us? How will that impact our corporate culture and our strategies for generating shareholder value?

The costs of not asking those questions are huge. If you're paying $2 million a month in real estate, then that is more or less fixed. It's an easy number to calculate. But what is the cost of having a workforce that is 60 percent Japanese (for example) and when you ask them to do something, they don't do it? Without cultural due diligence, you won't know what is holding them back or why. Remember Carlos Ghosn of Nissan?

There is no doubt that Japan handled the situation awfully, but if there is criticism against Ghosn, it is that he forgot which country he was operating in. "Any global chief executive has to be sensitive to political nuance," the BBC writes. "The fact that Carlos Ghosn, after nearly 20 years at Nissan, was totally blindsided by his arrest in Tokyo suggests he had lost touch with the organizations he was trying to bring closer together."[92]

In global corporations and cross-cultural situations, leaders must be attuned to the nuances of the society they are operating in. We are not suggesting leaders compromise their morals, only that they adjust and be sensitive to cultural expectations and political nuance. This is why consistent cultural due diligence is a must, and good leaders prioritize it in companies committed to sustainability and positive change.

Leaders who admit to their mistakes, commit to SDGs and ESG strategies, perform cultural due diligence, and reach for sustainability will see that movement gain momentum. The company will be able to hire better employees as a result. Their cost of capital will go down, and it will be cheaper for them to do business. Their human capital will improve, and they'll move in a direction that will, in the end, make all of them winners.

The next step for leadership isn't an internal town hall meeting every six months where the CEO offers a diatribe about how wonderful things are going, or how badly, but how everything will work out fine if everyone sticks together and works hard. The right direction requires talking about what the company is doing well, where they're falling down, and how leadership is holding themselves accountable for setting the tone going for-

---

92 Dearbail Jordan and Simon Jack, "Ex-Nissan Boss Carlos Ghosn: How I Escaped Japan in a Box," *BBC News*, July 13, 2021, https://www.bbc.com/news/business-57760993.

ward. It might require training programs for management and employees. It might require letting people go who are holding the company back.

A leader who isn't equipped to transform their business from a traditional one with problems around the environment, society, governance, human rights, and other topical issues can reach out to outside sources. Coaches, speakers, and consultants who specialize in management best practices can make a substantial difference.

If you want to know where you currently stand in this regard, ask your people. Offer an anonymous survey to your employees. Ask your partners and customers for their feedback too. Like Abigail Johnson did, you may have to bring in third-party professionals to ensure objectivity and also to protect employees. If you don't do this, employees will be hesitant to open up about what they're experiencing. For example, one company had a harassment hotline on their homepage that connected an employee to the company's HR division. The human resources person would take the complaint and immediately inform the employee's manager to squeal on the person, who would then get harassed further.

This process has been standard procedure at many companies for generations. HR is in place to protect the company, not the people. For many years, their job has been to keep a lid on internal issues and assist in helping anyone who complained out the door. Again, this is why engaging a third party can benefit the company in the long run. An outside lawyer will listen to complaints and manage them objectively; they have no allegiance to the company. Likewise, management can put in place whistleblower protection programs. A person has to feel comfortable raising their hand when they see a problem, and not have to worry about being punished or ostracized or losing their job.

Third-party evaluations are essential to breaking down unsustainable practices in an organization. It forces an organization to be answerable to something other than its own internal system. That external pressure is instrumental in creating change. Without it, corporations and systems (like Japan, Inc.) remain above criticism—in a way, untouchable. As Karel van Wolferen says,

> There being thus nothing outside the System to overrule or judge it, the System can only judge itself. This means that it is intrinsically virtuous, and that criticism of its essence is impossible; its guardians confirm this when they insist that the order they represent is inherently benevolent. In this way, the System also becomes a substitute for religion.[93]

If you insist on keeping your checks and evaluations limited to internal departments in your company, like HR, then you risk creating a corporation that believes itself to be a religion—in other words, above any true reproach. The consequences of this, ultimately, are defeat, for either your employees will be too scared to speak up or, when they do speak up, they'll be shown the door for daring to criticize the system. What you'll get is another Enron, hurtling down the track at full speed and no one around to pull the brakes, even though there's a cliff right ahead of you.

It's also important to have your policies written down in black and white—and make sure you adhere to them. Abigail Johnson made it clear to her company that harassment wouldn't be tolerated, and then she acted on it. She made it a part of the company culture. Cement your intentions—whether that be a

---

93   van Wolferen, *Enigma of Japanese Power*, 273.

zero harassment policy or a whistleblower protection program—into a written rulebook that you clearly follow. This is one way to guard against the effect of corporations as religion, for the rulebook can act as a force to dispel this notion of religion. In other words, it can be used to correct course, and make sure your company is on a sustainable path.

Leadership may have called issues "one-off" problems in the past, and then buried them, expecting them to disappear. But you can't bury a problem and hope the bones never come up again. Bad behavior is seldom a one-time occurrence, and if it's allowed one time, it will continue to happen. The interconnectedness of the world guarantees that it won't be kept secret either. Think of these types of problems as weeds in a garden—if you leave one to grow, there will be five weeds the next day, and twenty-five the day after that. Weeds don't take care of themselves or suddenly go away.

Leaders can be more public about problems they're faced with and can talk openly about what they're doing to correct them. People want to hear that you're trying. They want to know that becoming a better company is important to you. They want to be invited to help you too, with questions, suggestions, and recommendations. Starting that conversation with your people and the public creates a positive circle of trust that becomes part of your corporate story. It shows some vulnerability, which is also an important step of trust and lays the groundwork for change. It becomes a topic of conversation around the water cooler and the coffee machine at work, among your customers, and online. You'll have a story of how you're doing more to do better, instead of a story about how you buried all the bad problems at your business and expected no one to notice.

When you can do all of that, you can pin the SDG badge on your lapel. You can tell your people that the company is changing for the better, beginning with you. Remember, action and transparency are what count. Empty talk and lies mean nothing; power and credit go to those leaders who try, and keep trying, to be better. In the words of Theodore Roosevelt:

> It is not the critic who counts; not the man who points out how the strong man stumbles or where the doer of deeds could have done them better. The credit belongs to the man who is actually in the arena, whose face is marred by dust and sweat and blood; who strives valiantly; who errs, who comes up short again and again, because there is no effort without error or shortcoming; but who does actually strive to do the deeds; who knows the great enthusiasms, the great devotions; who spends himself in a worthy cause; who at the best knows in the end the triumph of high achievement, and who at the worst, if he fails, at least fails while daring greatly, so that his place shall never be with those cold and timid souls who neither know victory nor defeat.[94]

When you transform your business this way, you may never want to leave it, but if you do, your prospects will be much improved. Large corporations look for CEOs who are great leaders and know how to make a company profitable. Today, they also want leaders who think beyond short-term share price performance. That emphasis is shifting, and CEOs who can bring sustainability and long-term growth to a business are more attractive.

---

94 Theodore Roosevelt, "Address at the Sorbonne in Paris, France: 'Citizenship in a Republic'," April 23, 1910," The American Presidency Project, accessed January 31, 2023, https://www.presidency.ucsb.edu/documents/address-the-sorbonne-paris-france-citizenship-republic.

KEY TAKEAWAY

Nippon Life Insurance Co. recently announced that, going forward, they would evaluate all their investments and loans according to ESG criteria. This Japanese insurance giant, worth 70 trillion yen in assets like stocks, bonds, and real estate, believes it will "improve investment returns...by increasing positions in companies with high ESG ratings. These companies are believed to be superior in management transparency."[95]

Nippon Life's decision wasn't based on altruism but on a clear understanding that doing the right thing is actually going to make you money. They are essentially returning to the heart of capitalism by putting their money into corporations that produce outsized profits while contributing extraordinary value to society. That's a monumental revolutionary shift coming from a major investor, and an acceptance of how the wind is blowing. "The way we lead in 2021 is not the way we're going to have to lead in 2026," as Michael Useem says, and the same holds true for today—what worked in 1980 won't work in this market.[96] Unsustainable management practices *will* lead to defeat—they simply won't create profit.

To be a good leader, you must lead your organization into the future, and that means adopting the management practices we describe in this book. Remember, the hallmarks of an unsustainable organization (or a company, country, or culture) are a system that cannot handle criticism, that refuses to change, and that is guided by an "overriding, sacrosanct aim": its survival.[97]

---

95   Pedro Gonçalves, "Japan's Nippon Life to Adopt ESG Evaluation for All Investments," International Investment, October 21, 2020, https://www.internationalinvestment.net/news/4022065/japan-nippon-life-adopt-esg-evaluation-investments.

96   Knowledge at Wharton Staff, "Learning to Be a Better Leader."

97   van Wolferen, *Enigma of Japanese Power*, 433.

If you see these warning signs in your corporation, it's time to correct course.

The message that Nippon Life Insurance Co. sent out into the world should act as a call to action. It should be ringing alarm bells throughout corporate boardrooms around the world. Companies who are listening should be getting the message loud and clear: to be profitable, you must be sustainable. Take better care of the world and the people in it, or you won't be getting any capital. Major investors will steer clear of your company.

GUIDED REFLECTIONS:

1. Who are the great leaders in your company?

....

2. What are the characteristics of the ideal leader in your cor-poration?

....

3. What leadership training programs does your company do and who is selected to participate? Why?

....

4. What is the incentive structure in your corporation?

....

5. Do you have a whistleblower protection program? How does it work?

....

6. Do you have a third-party independent management audit?

....

7. If you could employ anyone to come and be a leader at your company, who would you bring in and why?

....

8. If a journalist spent six months at your company, what would be the headline of the article they would write about the experience? Why? What would you want the headline to be?

....

CONCLUSION

"An eternal, positive and profitable ripple is created by a single act of caring."

—GLEN WOOD

If you began this book thinking that Sustainable Profitability Strategies, SDGs, or sustainability in business were passing fads, I sincerely hope that we've proved you wrong. Sustainability is in fact the heart of business and has been since the beginning of time.

No one starts a company planning for it to die. You create a company because you believe it's a great ongoing concern that is not only going to generate great profit, but also going to add value to society. You plan for it to expand, to serve a good purpose in the world, and to generate money for its stakeholders. No one takes on a leadership role in an organization planning for its demise. You want it to flourish and grow. You want to see your shareholders happy, your customers satisfied, your employees' lives improved. You want everyone to do well, and for the company to go from strength to strength.

All new ventures are begun from this position of longevity—the whole start of a business has always been about sustainability. It's a concept that has been around for thousands of years.

Today, in our society and our global way of thinking, sustainability has come front and center in separating good businesses from the bad. Capitalism wasn't always about only quarterly profits. The original foundation of capitalism is, as we've mentioned, corporations that are competitively able to generate outsized profits while adding extraordinary value to society. The word "sustainability" seems to be used without actually contemplating its meaning or the implications of identifying with it. Over the past few decades, we've strayed far from that foundational meaning of capitalism. Now we're coming back full circle to capitalism's original intent—and we're using sustainability as a marker to divide the "sheep" from the "goats."

This matters to every leader in the world today because it determines whether or not your company survives. Do you want to be a sheep or a goat? Do you want to be considered a great and upcoming organization, or would you rather be considered "unsustainable"? And if you'd rather be considered unsustainable (status quo), then by definition you're going to fail. You won't be around to matter.

But if you do want to survive and if a strong and sustainable corporation is your goal, then you need to rethink how you're going about that. Regardless of your motivations—selfish or altruistic, whether you're thinking about your company balance sheet or about the betterment of the world—you need sustainable management practices. That's what we've given you in this book: the different areas you need to look at to become a company of tomorrow, and some very serious questions to answer about your business and management practices. We want to help leaders around the world focus on the right things and ask the right questions, because not many people are.

ASK THE RIGHT QUESTIONS: WHAT'S REAL AND WHAT'S NOT?

A few years ago, I was waiting outside the Haneda Airport in Tokyo, Japan when a taxi from the Kokusai Taxi Company pulled up. I got in and the taxi driver asked me, "Where to?" Now *kokusai* in Japanese means "international." The name of this company translates exactly into "international taxi company." So I said, "New York, please."

It was a joke obviously, and the taxi driver and I laughed about it. Because Kokusai Taxi Company is definitely a local taxi company that operates domestically, no matter what it calls itself. When Japan went through the economic boom of the 80s and businesses were growing rapidly, everything was called *kokusai-ka* or "internationalization" whether or not the company was international. It was this pure desire to *look* international, regardless of the reality.

Let me give you another example. We've had Chinese food in the US for decades now. Some of those restaurants are run by Chinese people, some of them are not. But the fact is, there's very little Chinese about the Chinese food you get in the US. It may be called "Chinese," but the food doesn't reflect the cuisine of China much at all. They're new dishes shaped to suit American tastes (loaded with sugar and fat for the most part).

Throughout this book, we've talked about companies that use language of this kind to mask their real commitments. They pay lip service to ESG strategies and claim to care about SDGs but they adopt practices and actions that directly contradict those seventeen United Nations' goals. Like the taxi company that chose a name that doesn't reflect what it does at all, these companies have been pretending to be something they're not.

So now, at the end of this book, I want you to take a step back and ask yourself: What's real? What's not? What does genuine progress look like, and what is hollow performance? And which kind of future do you want to foster? The taxi company and the Chinese restaurants are funny examples of what is real and what is not, but when you've got corporations firing pregnant women, that's not funny. You can laugh about the fact that your sweet and sour chicken balls are fake Chinese, but the rest of what is in this book—that's no laughing matter.

Ask yourself these questions and find answers that guide you towards sustainability. Remember, the right questions can be very powerful. As Tony Robbins said: "Quality questions create a quality life. Successful people ask better questions, and as a result, they get better answers." That is why we have a list of questions at the end of each chapter. Ask empowering questions and take massive action towards your goals.

We're not trying to manipulate people to some outcome with these queries—we're trying to empower you to think about things you may not have considered, so that you can find better solutions and ways of functioning in this new world. If you take this book seriously, and answer those questions sincerely, then we believe it will have a very positive impact not only on your life and on your family's life, but on your business and all its stakeholders. You will, by definition, be embracing success, not embracing defeat.

Awful as the recent COVID-19 pandemic was, it has given us a chance to reset how we do things. As Paul Krugman writes: "The pandemic was deadly and costly, but one small compensation is that it gave us a chance to think, work and live differently."[98] All that remains now is to seize that chance and make the most of it.

For here's the bald truth: organizations that don't embrace sustainability will find themselves obsolete in a few years. There may be businesses in today's world that are too big to fail, thanks to how the courts support them and the governments protect them. But I would argue that as the world changes towards a more sustainable outlook, the end of these businesses is very, very near. In our new world, there's no such thing as too big to care.

NEXT STEPS

If you haven't gone through the questions at the end of each chapter, I highly encourage you to read them and answer in full. They will help you think about where you are as a leader and a business, and what your next steps might be.

If you enjoyed what you read here and want to continue the conversation, head over to https://smartvisionlogistics.com/book/. There, we feature blogs with updated information on ESG strategies, SDGs, and the latest trends in this sustainable, globalized world. We provide a bibliography of resources cited in this book and a bibliography featuring additional resources. And, of course, we have provided our contact information. Tell us what you are thinking and connect with like-minded individuals on the same journey as you.

For people who don't know where to even start when it comes to sustainability, SVL Logistics is here to help. If you

---

98   Paul Krugman, "Working Out: Alexander Hamilton and Post-Covid America," *The New York Times*, July 2, 2021, https://www-nytimes-com.cdn.ampproject.org/c/s/www.nytimes.com/2021/07/02/opinion/work-jobs-employment.amp.html.

think it will be useful, feel free to contact us. We are happy to visit with you and your leadership, and we offer one-on-one consultations.

ACKNOWLEDGMENTS

Thank you to...

Mom, for being the ultimate educator and "the leader of the band."

Dr. Frederick Schmidt, for being an incredible mentor, guide, and friend, and for critiquing the book.

Tatsuhiko Nakazawa, for being an awesome friend, brother, and business partner.

My friends and family, for all your support, guidance, and love over the years.

Jeff Clark, for your friendship, guidance, advice—not to mention being the ultimate pastry chef!

David Wagner, for your friendship, coaching, and teaching.

David Russell, for your friendship, guidance, constant support, and for being a faithful advisor.

Fumiko Mochida, for being an incredible mother and advocate every step of the way.

Yumiko Nakajima and the Union, for your undying support and wisdom as we uncover non-sustainable corporate actions at Mitsubishi and Morgan Stanley.

My lawyers, the incredible attorneys that have been faithfully and intelligently guiding me and taking action against non-sustainable behaviors at Mitsubishi and Morgan Stanley: Mr. Imaizumi, Mr. Takano, Mrs. Yoshida, Mr. Enatsu, and Mr. Yamaguchi.

The many supporters at Mitsubishi and at Morgan Stanley who have remained faithful and true over the years. I couldn't have continued without all your support and friendship.

Brian Anderson at Fathering Together for all your friendship, support, and all the work you do to help fathers become better.

Tony Robbins, for your teaching, guidance, advice, and mentorship over the past thirty-five years. You set my life on a new course, and I am forever grateful.

Michael Steinberg, for being the best boss I ever had. I will never forget all you have done for me.

Stephen Kagawa, for being a true brother, mentor, and business partner.

Lester Fretz, for being a supportive teacher, mentor, and friend for most of my life. I miss you my dear friend.

ABOUT THE AUTHORS

GLEN WOOD has more than twenty-five years of experience across both Fortune 500 companies and governmental think-tanks, including Goldman Sachs, Mitsubishi UFJ Morgan Stanley, and the Japanese Council of Local Authorities for International Relations. He's made regular TV appearances on CNN, CNBC, BBC, Nikkei, and Aljazeera as an economics expert, and has directly advised the former Prime Minister of Japan, Ryutaro Hashimoto, on the educational and financial systems in the country. Today, he's the president and co-founder of Smart Vision Logistics (SVL), a company born from his commitment to the sustainable future of business and a return to the heart of capitalism. Glen is passionate about saving corporations that otherwise would not survive the upcoming transformation in the marketplace, boasting a remarkable track record that proves his unwavering dedication to clients.

Glen's story with Mitsubishi UFJ Morgan Stanley has created waves around the world, featuring in more than one hundred media outlets and translated into dozens of languages. He has been dubbed the "father of Japan" for his bravery and outspokenness on paternal rights, and his story has inspired thousands of fathers to stand up for themselves. He continues advocating for paternal rights, human rights, and women in leadership through his philanthropy efforts and conversations on television, talk shows, podcasts, and investing activities.

An MBA graduate from Wharton, Glen is an active member of the Pacific Council on International Policy, the US–Japan Council, and the Harvard Program on International Financial Systems. He travels extensively, dividing most of his time between Canada, the US and Japan, but calls Tokyo home. You can find him on LinkedIn, Facebook, and Twitter.

TATSUHIKO NAKAZAWA is the CEO and co-founder of Smart Vision Logistics (SVL), a pioneering company revolutionizing the global landscape with circular economics. He believes in the power of the people to transform businesses from the inside out and is dedicated to helping corporations harness the power of circles to grow and become competitive in this fast-evolving, newly sustainable world.

Previously the founder and CEO of TrustOne Logistics Corporation and with more than twenty-five years of experience in his field, Tatsuhiko has built a reputation as a trusted leader in the Japanese business community. He has a high sense of innovation and great entrepreneurial spirit and enjoys working with growth-minded leaders across the globe. He lives in Chichibu, Japan, and travels the globe much of the year.

www.ingramcontent.com/pod-product-compliance
Lightning Source LLC
Chambersburg PA
CBHW031841200326
41597CB00012B/229